BRUCE WEBER'S
★ **INSIDE** ★
BASEBALL
◇ 1990 ◇

SCHOLASTIC INC.
New York Toronto London Auckland Sydney

PHOTO CREDITS

Cover: Photo of Bo Jackson/Focus on Sports. **iv, 18, 22, 74:** San Francisco Giants. **3, 14, 28, 44:** Kansas City Royals. **4, 11, 32:** Milwaukee Brewers. **6, 34:** Toronto Blue Jays. **7, 40:** New York Yankees. **8, 13, 15, 46:** Oakland Athletics. **9, 38** (left): Baltimore Orioles. **10, 27, 48** (left), **50:** Minnesota Twins. **12, 52, 84:** Texas Rangers. **16, 23, 72** (left): San Diego Padres. **19, 25, 64:** Chicago Cubs. **20, 60:** New York Mets. **21, 24, 76:** Cincinnati Reds. **26, 58, 80:** Houston Astros. **30:** Boston Red Sox. **36, 72** (right): Cleveland Indians. **38** (right), **68:** Philadelphia Phillies. **42:** Detroit Tigers. **48** (right), **54:** Seattle Mariners. **56, 62** (left): Chicago White Sox. **62** (right), **78:** Los Angeles Dodgers. **66:** Pittsburgh Pirates. **70:** Montreal Expos. **82:** Atlanta Braves.

ISBN 0-590-43463-2

12 11 10 9 8 7 6 5 4 3 2 1   0 1 2 3 4 5/9

Printed in the U.S.A.   01

First Scholastic printing, April 1990

CONTENTS

Phillie Von Hayes is doubled up by Giant
2B Robby Thompson. It'll be more of the
same in '90: San Fran up; Philly down.

THE MONEY GAME

Used to be that you couldn't tell the ball-players without a scorecard. These days you can't tell the players without their agents, their accountants, their tax advisers, and the public-relations men.

Can you imagine? Boss Steinbrenner paid nearly six million bucks for Montreal's flakiest pitcher, Pascual Perez. The Twins laid nine million for three years at the feet of Kirby Puckett. The Cards attracted Bryn Smith with their two million bucks for each of three years. Next came Oakland's $12 million for four years of Rickey Henderson. Kansas City will pay Mark Davis $13 million for four years. And then, unbelievably, the Angels signed Mark Langston to a five-year contract for $16 million.

Incredible! Six million. Twelve million. Sixteen million. Does it make sense? An accountant could present an excellent case. Simply, money in sports doesn't mean a thing.

Television is one culprit. When CBS paid one *billion* dollars for seven years of the NCAA basketball tournament, all bets were off.

Basically the value of anything is exactly what someone is willing to pay for it. If Rickey Henderson, who tends to flounder when he's comfortable, is worth three mill a year for four years, then any previous money figures fly out the window. Steinbrenner's 1.9 mill a year for Perez, who was 9–13 with a 3.31 ERA for Montreal in '89, changed every standard for pitchers.

Who pays for all of this? You do, of course. When club owners pay higher salaries, ticket prices rise. Maybe not this year, but one day the fan pays. When TV networks pay a billion dollars for game rights, their commercial prices rise. When companies pay $1.4 million for a one-minute Super Bowl commercial, they pass the cost on to their customers.

Meanwhile, back on the field where money doesn't mean a thing, things should be as exciting as ever.

Seems like the Cubs, with a year's experience, should get better, but that might not be good enough. With a couple of healthy pitchers, the Cardinals and the ever-present Mets should be right up there. San Diego may well catch the Giants in '90, though another expensive free agent, Kevin Bass, improves San Fran's chances.

If Henderson doesn't go to sleep and Jose Canseco stays out of trouble, the A's should repeat in the AL West. The Brewers, if they settle their problems on the left side of the infield, could well catch the Blue Jays.

With trades continuing hot and heavy as we go to press, maybe we'll need that scorecard after all. In the meantime, have fun while you can afford it.

— Bruce Weber
December 1989

BO JACKSON
KANSAS CITY ROYALS

Bo knows a lot of things. You know he knows baseball. Of course he knows football. He can probably learn hockey with a little practice. And he certainly knows how to make money.

Vincent Edward Jackson is probably the USA's most talented athlete. He's big (6–1, 225 pounds), he's strong, he runs like the wind, he jumps, he hits baseballs over buildings, he throws home on the fly from the warning track. We don't know if he can walk on water, but if the waterfall at Royals Stadium overflows, we may find out.

Yup, Bo knows lots of things. What he doesn't know yet is the strike zone, though the Royals aren't overly concerned. Auburn's Heisman Trophy winner captured everyone's attention with his monster leadoff homer off Rick Reuschel in the July '89 All-Star game. He was the game's leading vote-getter going in; he was the game's MVP going out. Overall, he led Kaycee with 86 runs, 32 homers, 105 RBIs, and a .495 slugging percentage. He also topped the Royals with 172 strikeouts.

Bo also knows his athletic career could end in a flash as he totes the ball for the LA Raiders every fall. It makes the Royals crazy, but Bo loves it.

At age 34, 16-year Brewer vet Robin Yount
has never been better, which made him a
hot topic on the winter free-agent trail.

American League ALL-PRO TEAM

First Base
FRED McGRIFF
TORONTO BLUE JAYS

Things weren't going very well in Toronto last spring. The Blue Jays had lost 30 of their first 50 games. They switched ballparks. They switched managers. They were going nowhere. There was only one bright spot — Fred McGriff. He was hitting the ball out of sight (11 homers in the first six weeks), to keep the Jays breathing — barely.

The rest, as they say, is history. Under new manager Cito Gaston, Toronto turned it around and won the AL East title — thanks largely to the 26-year-old McGriff. The Tampa native starts his fourth big-league campaign with the 1989 AL home-run title (36) behind him. The rest of his '89 numbers included 92 RBIs, 98 runs scored, and 119 walks.

More important, the threat of McGriff renewed the baseball life of left fielder George Bell. Seeing the 6–3, 215-pound McGriff in the on-deck circle forced AL pitchers to groove the ball to Bell. That may have cut down on McGriff's RBIs (Bell got 104 runners home), but helped win a championship for the Blue Jays.

Though Seattle's Alvin Davis and New York's Don Mattingly hit for higher averages and had more RBIs, our vote goes to Toronto's big man.

Second Base
STEVE SAX
NEW YORK YANKEES

Fans of Texas's Julio Franco may argue, but our choice for the AL's best at second base is Steve Sax. With his fine performance last season, he had already convinced Yankee fans that he's the best.

Few players handle pressure like the former Dodger. He arrived in New York to replace one of the most popular Yankees ever: Willie Randolph. And Big Apple fans still had nightmares about Sax's throwing arm, which often deposited bad throws to first into the third row of the box seats at Dodger Stadium.

Forget it. The Sacramento (CA) native won over the New York crowd immediately. He hit early and often, even when Don Mattingly was slumping early in the season. The eight-year veteran pounded the ball at a .315 clip for the year, only his second .300-plus season in the majors. The one-time NL Rookie of the Year hit .332 for the 1986 Dodgers.

With his defense straightened out, the timely hitting Sax is heading toward the prime of his career. If he can avoid injury and the public pressures that seem to build for many of the Bronx Brombers, he should be the Yankee second baseman for years to come.

Third Base
CARNEY LANSFORD
OAKLAND ATHLETICS

Carney Lansford can flat out hit. He has been doing it in the big leagues since 1979. In fact, he led the AL in hitting in 1981 (.336) as the Red Sox third baseman. Then Wade Boggs arrived, and Lansford was dispatched to Oakland. Even at age 33, Carney can still hit.

What's more, the one-time Santa Clara (CA) schoolboy star has discovered previously unknown speed. From 1982 to 1985, the 6-2, 195-pounder stole 23 bases — total. Then in 1986 Lansford caught the speed bug. He stole 16 bases that year, 27 in '87, 29 in '88, and a career-high 37 in '89. Amazing!

In 1988 Lansford was hitting over .400 in early June. A late slump, however, dropped his final numbers to .279. But '89 was a different story. Lansford hit all year and finished at .336, trailing only Minnesota's Kirby Puckett.

Choosing the AL All-Pro third baseman isn't easy. The game's best hitter, Boston's Boggs, hangs out at the hot corner. Kansas City's Kevin Seitzer is a front liner all the way. Minnesota's Gary Gaetti should bounce back in '90. And Toronto's Kelly Gruber is a comer. But we'll stick with Lansford, the oldster with the young legs.

Shortstop
CAL RIPKEN
BALTIMORE ORIOLES

As a shortstop, Cal Ripken has limited range. That's his weakness — his only weakness. He makes up for it with great hands and an outstanding arm.

That's the book on the Orioles' superstar. In every other department, he excels. He hits a ton, knocks in runs, hits with power, makes good contact, and leads the ball club on and off the field. When Baltimore bounced back from the majors' worst record in 1988 to a near-miss for the AL East title in '89, it was Ripken who set the tone.

Son of former Bird manager and current coach Cal Sr. and brother of DP mate Billy, Cal Jr. is the perfect man for manager Frank Robinson to have on the field. And he's on the field every day. Since May 30, 1982, he has been in 1,250 straight games. Only ex-Yankees Everett Scott and Iron Horse Lou Gehrig stand ahead in this category. If he stays healthy, he'll catch the leader, Gehrig, in June 1995.

His 21 homers marked his eighth straight year with 20 or more. That tied Hall-of-Famer Ernie Banks's all-time mark. He also hit .257, banged out 30 doubles, and knocked in a team-leading 93 runs.

Like manager Robinson, we'll write Ripken on our lineup card every day.

9

Outfield
KIRBY PUCKETT
MINNESOTA TWINS

Here's a plug for Kirby Puckett. He's built like a fireplug (5–8, 210 pounds) and plays like a flashy spark plug. If anything happens to Puckett, you can pull the plug on the Twins.

Easily one of the most exciting players in the game, Puckett plays with amazing intensity. He hits everything — to all fields. His .339 batting average led the majors (after his .356 mark in '88 was good for only second in the AL). He also smashed 45 doubles among his 215 hits. Though his power slipped a bit (nine homers), he still knocked in 85 runs.

The 29-year-old is just as good in the outfield. He's extremely quick and gets to balls that normal humans take on one hop. It's amazing to watch the little guy get up like an NBA rebounder to snatch enemy home runs from the far side of the Metrodome fence.

Best of all, Kirby is durable. His 635 at-bats in '89 marked his fifth straight year with 600 or more ABs. And his 215 hits marked his fourth straight year at 200 or more, rare for a right-handed hitter. Interestingly, his stolen bases have slipped from a high of 21 in 1985 to only 11 last year. Has manager Tom Kelly put up the "stop" sign?

ROBIN YOUNT
Milwaukee Brewers

After 16 years in the majors, most players are looking to coast home. Not Robin Yount. The 34-year-old Yount hit the big time as a Milwaukee shortstop in 1974 at the tender age of 18. He quickly became the guy who made the Brew Crew go — and still is.

The year he had in '89 was tremendous by anyone's standards. But for Yount, it was just a bit better than usual. His .318 batting average was good for fourth in the league. And he banged in 103 runs, which kept the Brewers in the pennant chase longer than they deserved to be.

The 6–0, 180-pounder was also in double figures in almost every offensive category — with 38 doubles, 9 triples, and 21 homers. In fact, the only offensive area in which he did not excel was bases-on-balls received (63). Since the other Brewers weren't exactly major power threats, who could blame the hot-hitting Yount for taking his hacks.

While Yount makes the most noise at the plate, what makes him an All-Pro is his all-around play. He's excellent defensively, runs the bases well, and leads the ball club on and off the field. When will this stop? Nobody knows. Robin Yount shows no signs of age!

RUBEN SIERRA
TEXAS RANGERS

If the Texas Rangers ever put together a season, maybe everyone will know about Ruben Sierra. He's one of the American League's best-kept secrets.

You have to see this guy to believe him. Because the Rangers have been terrible, no one ever thinks about putting a Texas game on national TV. Too bad.

Puerto Rico native Sierra has been compared to Puerto Rico's most famous baseball son, the late Roberto Clemente. Nice company. Sierra will never hit like Clemente did, but Clemente would be jealous of Sierra's power and speed. His 29 homers last season gave him 98 before his 24th birthday (October 6, 1989). Only baseball's most famous sluggers have done better. More important, Sierra hit .306 in '89, 42 points better than his previous career high.

There's no telling how good the 6–1, 175-pounder can be. His numbers get better every year. He banged in a league-leading 119 runs for the so-so Rangers last season, topping his previous career high of 109. In addition to his 29 round-trippers, he smacked 35 doubles and 14 triples, for a .543 slugging average. Scouts look for players who can hit, hit with power, field, run, and throw. Sierra does 'em all!

Catcher
TERRY STEINBACH
OAKLAND ATHLETICS

This is the American League's Social Security position. Seems like half of the AL's catchers are eligible for the senior citizens' league. Imagine 42-year-olds like Carlton Fisk and Bob Boone, and 38-year-old Ernie Whitt, still out there almost every day.

That's why our choice for AL All-Pro backstop goes to the man of 1990 — and beyond — Oakland's Terry Steinbach.

Steinbach was a surprise starter and even more surprising MVP of the 1988 All-Star game (he was hitting .217 at the time). But he hit .297 the rest of the way and finished at .265. Last year he raised the numbers to .273, with seven homers and 42 RBIs. His offense was never really in question. His defense was another story. But the former college third baseman (U. of Minnesota) continues to improve behind the plate. He has the tools; the rest will come with experience.

Minnesota's Brian Harper is a better hitter than Steinbach, but Harper can't get the job done defensively. Though Terry's RBIs slipped from 56 and 51 in 1987 and '88, he plays an important role in the fearsome lineup that manager Tony LaRussa sends to the plate.

BRET SABERHAGEN
KANSAS CITY ROYALS

Poor Dave Stewart. All he does is win 20 or more every year, and someone else always edges him for the Cy Young Award. In '89 it was the Royals' Bret Saberhagen who closed with an incredible rush.

Saberhagen's performance shouldn't surprise anyone. He has always been outstanding in odd-numbered years (20–6 in 1985, 18–10 in 1987). So his fabulous 1989 (23–6, 2.16 ERA, 193 strikeouts, 12 complete games) won him his second Cy Young Award.

A young veteran at age 26 (on April 11), the Royals' right-hander is one of baseball's top control pitchers. In '89 he walked 43 batters in 262 innings. For his career, he's the only active big-leaguer allowing fewer than two walks per nine innings. Meanwhile his 193 K's were a personal best.

The key to 1990 is Saberhagen's preparation. In the past, Bret has followed a great season with a soft off-season and a mediocre next-season. Now after six big-league years, Saberhagen has matured. There's simply nothing that he can't accomplish on the mound. If he finally understands that — and if his support increases at Kansas City — he could be in the All-Pro picture into the year 2000.

DAVE STEWART
OAKLAND ATHLETICS

A bunch of major-league scouts have to be kicking themselves. In May 1986, right-hander Dave Stewart was a free agent. Cut by the Phillies after eight relief performances (and a 6.57 ERA), Stewart was listening to offers. There weren't many.

When the A's called, Stewart was thrilled to go home — to Oakland. For starters, manager Tony LaRussa sent his new man out to face Boston's then-unbeatable Roger Clemens on national TV. Stewart won and hasn't looked back.

No other active big-league pitcher has strung together three straight 20-win seasons. And while Stewart hasn't won a Cy Young Award yet, he has managed to cash his share of postseason checks. (Would you believe $114,000 for the '89 World Series?)

What makes Stewart so valuable is his consistency. He goes out there every five days and gets it done. His 21–9 record in '89 followed years of 20–13 and 21–12. That's an average of 32 decisions every season, exactly what a manager looks for. True, Stewart gets plenty of support from Oakland's booming bats and steady bullpen. Still, when you're looking for comeback heroes, focus on Dave Stewart, the pitcher nobody wanted.

Sweet-swinging Tony Gwynn (above), the NL's best pure hitter, gets help in '90 from Padre big sticks Jack Clark and Joe Carter.

National
League
ALL-PRO TEAM

First Base
WILL
CLARK
SAN FRANCISCO GIANTS

Ask Cub manager Don Zimmer. When you face the San Francisco Giants, you begin with Will Clark. You keep Brett Butler and Robby Thompson off the bases to reduce Clark's RBI potential. You change pitchers to get a lefty to face the awesome lefty. Sure you worry about Kevin Mitchell, but Clark is the guy who can kill you in so many ways.

A 1984 U.S. Olympic Team hero, following a superb All-America career at Mississippi State, Clark put in one year in the minors (65 games at Class A Fresno) before arriving to stay at Candlestick Park. He turned around a Nolan Ryan fastball for a homer in his first major-league at-bat. He has gone on from there.

His .333 bat mark (with 23 homers) was second best in the NL in '89. Only teammate Mitchell had more RBIs (125) than the 6–1, 190-pound Clark (111).

On defense he's equally gifted. He finished second in the NL in putouts, chances, and double plays.

Clark's weaknesses? According to "the book," he doesn't have any. You just make your pitch and hope he hits it to someone. The man whom they call "The Natural" is just that.

Second Base
RYNE
SANDBERG
CHICAGO CUBS

Chicago's famous Lincoln Park zoo has always housed the city's best-known rhino. Now there's a more popular Ryno on Chicago's north side. He's Ryne Sandberg, who gets it done at another Windy City zoo, Wrigley Field.

In '89 Sandberg enjoyed his best year since 1984, when he was the NL Most Valuable Player. He did it all. In the field, his record 90 straight errorless games earned him his seventh straight Gold Glove. No other NL second sacker has won as many as six straight. His speed produced 15 stolen bases. His .290 batting average was his best since '85.

But what separates Ryno from the rest of the All-Pro contenders is his power. Second basemen usually don't have any. Since California's Bobby Grich hammered 26 homers in 1979, no other 2B had matched that total. But Sandberg banged out 30 homers last season, including one superhot streak of six homers in five games in mid-August when the Cubs were making their run to the top of the NL East.

On a basically young ball club (rookies Walton, Smith, Wrona, and Girardi among them), Sandberg's leadership-by-example produces championships.

Third Base
HOWARD
JOHNSON
NEW YORK METS

A year ago, Howard Johnson had his bags packed. The only sure thing was that HoJo would be leaving the Mets — probably in a package for a frontline pitcher. The Mets never made the deal — and are they glad! Today Johnson is a Met untouchable.

There's still some doubt about Johnson's defense. There's still talk about playing him at shortstop, first base, left field, center field (choose one). After shoulder surgery in '88, he returned with one of the NL's stronger arms, though he has periods of wildness. But there's no doubt about his offense.

HoJo hit from opening day to closing day in '89, one of the few Mets to do so. He bounced back from a .230 bat mark in '88 to hit .287, his career high. He returned to the impressive 30–30 club for the second time in three years, smacking 36 homers (second only to Kevin Mitchell) and stealing 41 bases (third in the league). He may be ready to join Jose Canseco in the 40–40 club any year now. He banged out 41 doubles; tied for the league lead in runs scored (104); and slugged at a .559 clip, second best in the majors.

When Detroit manager Sparky Anderson dealt HoJo to the Mets, he said Howard would never make it. Sparky is slipping.

Shortstop
BARRY
LARKIN
CINCINNATI REDS

The old guard is changing. The Cards' Ozzie Smith was the NL's best shortstop for more than a decade. Rafael Ramirez fought the bad hops in Atlanta before moving on to Houston. San Diego's Garry Templeton was an artist.

Now a new bunch has arrived, featuring the Giants' Jose Uribe, the Mets' Kevin Elster, even Chicago's rifle-armed Shawon Dunston.

But the shortstop of the '90s is the Reds' Barry Larkin. Limited to only 97 games last year because of a freak injury at the All-Star game, hometown hero Larkin is ready to show the world in 1990. Had he managed to finish '89 the way he started it, he would have won the NL batting title. After finishing the '88 season with a 21-game hitting streak, he hit .342, with 111 hits and 36 RBIs in '89. The 25-year-old has a little power (four homers) and notched 10 steals in limited time.

Defense has never been his strongest suit, but it's getting better, much better, with experience. A natural athlete, Barry comes from an athletic family. While his brothers chose football and basketball for their college careers, everyone in Cincinnati is delighted that Barry picked baseball.

KEVIN MITCHELL
SAN FRANCISCO GIANTS

For years Kevin Mitchell has called himself "World," as in "All-World." For a man who had never hit more than .280 or 22 homers, it was a tough nickname to sell.

No more. The one-time Met and Padre got his whole act together in 1989. With teammate Will Clark, he helped form the best one-two punch in baseball.

At the plate, the 5–11, 210-pound Mitchell combines the key tools: strength and a quick bat. That combination produced a major-league leading 47 homers and 125 RBIs. Even when he's jammed, he manages to get the bat head out in front. When he makes good contact, the ball gets out of the park in a hurry. He also managed a career-high .291 batting average. And his slugging percentage of .635 was "world"-class (and 76 points better than runner-up Howard Johnson).

For years it looked like Mitchell would never make it. Signed by the Mets in 1980, he finally hit the big leagues in 1986, playing six positions for New York's world champs. Dealt to San Diego in late '86, he was quickly moved to San Francisco in July 1987. The arrival of 3B Matt Williams sent him to left field to stay, which is just dandy with the Giants' new superstar.

Outfield
TONY GWYNN
SAN DIEGO PADRES

Real baseball fans would pay serious money just to watch Tony Gwynn hit. He's got a gorgeous stroke, a superb eye, and great game sense. "All the tools," they say.

At age 29, Gwynn is at the top of his game. He was somewhat embarrassed when he won the 1988 NL bat title by hitting "only" .313. Not his style. His '87 numbers — .370 and 56 steals — were more like it.

The race to another hitting crown in 1989 was tough. Going into the last day of the season, he trailed the Giants' Will Clark (the Padres' opponent that day) by one point, .334 to .333. Tony had the answer. While Clark went one-for-four and slipped to .333, Gwynn had three singles in four trips to finish at .336.

With Jack Clark (26 homers) hitting behind him, Gwynn saw better pitches last season and sent many of them into places where fielders weren't located. He also recovered his touch on the bases, stealing 40, his second-best total ever.

The only shortcoming in Tony's game is power. Only once (1986) has he reached double figures in homers (14). But knowing that Tony will be on "the pond" much of the time (.389 on-base average) does nothing for Padre opponents' confidence.

Outfield
ERIC
DAVIS
CINCINNATI REDS

If Eric Davis ever gets to play a full season, watch out. He's averaging only 456 at-bats a season over the past four. Yet he still does amazing things at bat and in the field.

If he's ever going to have a full season, 1990 should be the year. It's his "walk" year. Unless he signs now for 1991 and beyond, he'll be available as a free agent after the '90 season. If money drives a pro, Davis is right behind the wheel.

Despite missing 31 games in '89, Davis posted more fabulous numbers. He stroked the ball at a .281 clip, not bad for a slugger. His 34 home runs trailed only Kevin Mitchell and Howard Johnson. He knocked in 101 runs (fourth in the league) and even stole 21 bases. Projected over 162 games, Davis would have hit 43 homers, banged in 126 runs, and stolen 26 bags. Not too shabby.

Davis is equally effective in the field. He has great range and a fine arm, and has brought back countless home runs from over the fence with his glove.

Davis's dreams for the future include playing on grass (instead of Cincy's artificial turf) and teaming up with childhood buddy Darryl Strawberry, another '90 free agent.

24

Catcher
DAMON BERRYHILL
CHICAGO CUBS

How good would the Cubs have been if Damon Berryhill had been healthy all year? Joe Girardi and Rick Wrona, up from Class AA, filled in nicely. But Berryhill's absence probably caused manager Don Zimmer to lose whatever hair he had left last summer.

At age 26, and after only one-and-a-half big-league seasons, Berryhill has earned enormous respect from NL rivals. Even after shoulder repair, he came back in 1989 and kept National League base runners at bay. In 1988, his only full big-league season, Berryhill gunned down 44 of 110 runners, a nifty 40% average.

Though he hit only .257, the switch-hitting southern-California native comes through in the clutch. He made his major-league debut on September 5, 1987, and banged a grand-slam homer on September 13. When he returned from the DL in May 1989, he smacked a 12th-inning homer to beat San Francisco.

For years, picking the NL All-Pro catcher was a breeze. Johnny Bench and Gary Carter dominated the position for years. Now it's a tough call. If Berryhill doesn't make it back from injury, watch Houston's Craig Biggio or a bounce-back effort from San Diego's Benito Santiago.

Pitcher
MIKE
SCOTT
HOUSTON ASTROS

Does he or doesn't he? No, it's not a hair-color commercial. It's a discussion of Mike Scott's pitching technique. National Leaguers are convinced that the Houston right-hander will rip, tear, gouge, or scuff a baseball before zipping it to the plate. Maybe he does or maybe he doesn't. Either way, he has NL batters thinking about it — and that has helped him become the league's toughest starter.

A one-time so-so Met (1979–82), Scott found himself in Astroland. Winning took a while. As late as 1984, he was a 5–11 pitcher. Then he learned the split-fingered fastball, possibly learned how to doctor the ball, and achieved immediate success. Good control and a solid 90-mph fastball made Scott a dominant pitcher.

He was never better than in Houston's near-miss season of '86 (18–10, 2.22 ERA, 306 strikeouts). But not until 1989 did Mike arrive in the 20-win circle, when he was the NL's only 20-game winner, going 20–10 for the NL West's third-place team. He had nine complete games, one off the league high. His 172 strikeouts, though his lowest total in four years, put him among the league's top 10. Pitching in a pitchers' park, Scott scares the daylights out of NL rivals.

FRANK VIOLA
NEW YORK METS

There are a couple of unwritten baseball rules: You can never be too rich and you can never have too much pitching, especially young pitching. When the New York Mets gave up five youthful arms to get Minnesota's Cy Young Award winner Frank Viola last summer, they hoped it would win them the 1989 NL East title. It didn't, but it might bring the flag to Shea in 1990.

Baseball's highest-paid pitcher until the free-agent dealings of the 1989–90 winter, Viola loves being back home in New York. He'd love it even more if the Mets would get him a few runs, something they failed to do in his two-month Shea stay in '89. New York scored two runs or fewer in four of the lefty's first five starts and in seven of his 12 starts.

Viola, who will be 30 on April 19, combines great control, excellent speed, fine location, and a good assortment of stuff. Forget '89. Forget the 0–5 start with the Twins and the 8–12 record before the trade. Forget the 5–5 mark with the Mets. The powerful 6–4, 209-pound Viola remains one of the game's top left-handers and, without the pressure of being the only stopper, he figures to get the job done for the home team every fifth day.

AL Cy Young winner Bret Saberhagen (above) could lead KC to the AL West title, with help from NL Cy Young winner Mark Davis.

American
League
TEAM PREVIEWS

AL East
BOSTON RED SOX
1989 Finish: Third
1990 Prediction: First

Dwight Evans

Roger Clemens

There are no fans more loyal than Boston Red Sox fans. But even the most loyal New Englander has to be worried about the home club. The pitching, after Roger Clemens, is shaky; the defense is weak; Nick Esasky bolted to Atlanta; and there isn't a dominant DH. Manager Joe Morgan has his work cut out.

Every major-league GM went shopping for his blockbuster deal in the Boston outfield. LF Mike Greenwell (.308, 95 RBIs) and CF Ellis Burks (.303, but only 97 games) attracted attention everywhere. At age 38, RF Dwight Evans (.285, 100 RBIs) remains one of the game's most consistent run-producers.

No matter what troubles surround him, 3B Wade Boggs (.330, 107 walks, .430 on-base average) can flat out hit. His defense has come on strong, too. With 1B Esasky (.277, 30 homers, 108 RBIs) gone, there's a big hole to fill. Carlos Quintana (.208) worked at first in winter ball. 2B Marty Barrett (.256) is solid in every phase of the game. SS Jody Reed (.288) will be back, too. Ex-Cardinal and Pirate C Tony Pena will help, especially on defense, raising questions about Rick Cerone and chasing Rich Gedman.

Clemens (17–11, 3.13) may not be the pitcher he was three years ago, but he's still the rock of the Bosox staff. RHP Bob Stanley retired, RHP Joe Price was released, and RHP Oil Can Boyd became the Montreal Expos' problem this winter. RHP Greg Harris (2–2) will be back, along with John Dopson (12–8), Mike Boddicker (15–11), and a variety of other contenders. Reliever Lee Smith (6–1, 25 saves, but a 3.57 ERA) gives way to the '80s best closer, Jeff Reardon. A renewed Wes Gardner (3–7) will set up for Reardon.

STAT LEADERS — 1989

BATTING

Average: Boggs, .330
Runs: Boggs, 113
Hits: Boggs, 205
Doubles: Boggs, 51*
Triples: Boggs, 7
Home Runs: Esasky, 30
RBIs: Esasky, 108
Stolen Bases: Burks, 21

PITCHING

Wins: Clemens, 17
Losses: Smithson, 14
Complete Games:
  Clemens, 8
Shutouts: Clemens, 3
Saves: Smith, 25
Walks: Clemens, 93
Strikeouts: Clemens, 230

*Led league.

AL East
MILWAUKEE BREWERS
1989 Finish: Fourth
1990 Prediction: Second

Paul Molitor   **Chris Bosio**

The Brewers aren't far from a serious bid
at an AL East title. There's a solid corps of
starting pitchers, if they're healthy. There's
the one-two combo of Robin Yount and Paul
Molitor, if the Brewers are able to re-sign the
multitalented Yount. And there's the pati-
ence and organization of a former school-
teacher, manager Tom Trebelhorn.

If lefty Teddy Higuera (9–6, 3.46) had been
sound all season, the Brew Crew might
have been closer than they were (eight
games behind). He's joined by young RHP
Jaime Navarro (7–8, 3.12), who got only one
run while he was pitching in seven of his
eight losses; RHP Chris Bosio (15–10, 2.95);
RHP Tom Filer (7–3, 3.61), and RHP Mark
Knudson (8–5, 3.35). It's a potentially solid
group. Add the bullpen, led by prime closer

Dan Plesac (3–4, 2.35, 33 saves), and the pitching is in decent shape.

3B Molitor (.315, 35 doubles) is the infield key, though he may be asked to play elsewhere in '90. SS Gary Sheffield (.247), the heralded 1989 rookie, gets another shot after a stay on the trading block, while Bill Spiers (.255) impressed a lot of folks in his rookie season. 1B Greg Brock (.265, 12 homers) has found a home in Wisconsin. 2B Jim Gantner (.274) and SS Dale Sveum (missed all of '89 and had shoulder surgery in November) try to bounce back.

At age 34, 16-year-vet CF Robin Yount continues to amaze (.318, 21 homers, 103 RBIs) on offense and defense. Young RF Greg Vaughn (.265) should become a starter at age 24. DHs Glenn Braggs (.247), an off-season trade subject, and Rob Deer (.210 and 158 strikeouts) are in trouble with the arrival of The Cobra, Oakland's Dave Parker. Charlie O'Brien (.234) and B.J. Surhoff (.248) will split the catching, with Obie the superior defensive player.

STAT LEADERS — 1989

BATTING
Average: Yount, .318
Runs: Yount, 101
Hits: Yount, 195
Doubles: Yount, 38
Triples: Yount, 9
Home Runs: Deer, 26
RBIs: Yount, 103
Stolen Bases: Molitor, 27

PITCHING
Wins: Bosio, 15
Losses: August, 12
Complete Games: Bosio, 8
Shutouts: Bosio, 2
Saves: Plesac, 33
Walks: August, 58
Strikeouts: Bosio, 173

AL East
TORONTO BLUE JAYS
1989 Finish: First
1990 Prediction: Third

Tony Fernandez   George Bell

With an eye toward another wide-open race in the AL East, you have to believe that the Toronto Blue Jays can repeat, though manager Cito Gaston shouldn't be looking for a cakewalk.

The Jays have plenty of plusses: deep pitching, excellent speed, and a generally productive lineup. They've got a few minuses, too: poor outfield defense, offensive mistakes, poor leadoff work.

They aren't Canseco and McGwire, but it's hard to argue with the Jays' one-two punch of George Bell and Fred McGriff. LF Bell hit .297 with 18 homers and 104 RBIs for the East champs in '89. 1B McGriff, possibly the AL's best, had 36 homers (but none after September 4, a major concern) and knocked in 92 runs. A pair of Dominicans,

Manny Lee (.260) and Nelson Liriano (.263), do a fine job splitting time at 2B, and Kelly Gruber (.290) has become a premier player at one of the AL's strongest positions, third base. They don't get any better than SS Tony Fernandez (.257).

With CF Lloyd Moseby (.221) off to Detroit, Gaston needs help in the leadoff spot. One candidate is RF Junior Felix (.258, 18 steals), who must capitalize on his speed. OFs Glenallen Hill and Chico Walker should get a shot. Neither catcher, Pat Borders (.257) or Ernie Whitt (.262), is a top-flight backstop.

The starting pitching is deep if not super-strong. Lefties Jimmy Key (13–14), Mike Flanagan (7–7), ex-Cub Paul Kilgus (6–10), and John Cerutti (11–11) join staff leader Dave Stieb (17–8, 3.35) and youngster Todd Stottlemyre (7–7) as game-openers. A healthy Al Leiter (only five games in '89) would help. They'll set up super reliever Tom Henke (8–3, 1.92, 20 saves) and Duane Ward (4–10 but 15 saves).

STAT LEADERS — 1989

BATTING
Average: Bell, .297
Runs: McGriff, 98
Hits: Bell, 182
Doubles: Bell, 41
Triples: Fernandez, 9
Home Runs: McGriff, 36*
RBIs: Bell, 104
Stolen Bases: Moseby, 24

PITCHING
Wins: Stieb, 17
Losses: Key, 14
Complete Games: Key, 5
Shutouts: Stieb, 2
Saves: Henke, 20
Walks: Stieb, 76
Strikeouts: Ward, 122

*Led league.

CLEVELAND INDIANS
1989 Finish: Sixth
1990 Prediction: Fourth

Tom Candiotti

Brook Jacoby

If the Baltimore Orioles can go from worst to nearly first, the Cleveland Indians reason, Why can't we? Indeed, why can't they, though we fail to see how.

Cleveland's new manager John McNamara has won before (he had the Red Sox within a Bill Buckner putout of a world title in 1986), but probably not with a group like this one. Slugger Joe Carter is off to San Diego, and it's unlikely that super-prospect C Sandy Alomar, Jr., or any of the other new Indians, can fill the gap — yet.

Meanwhile, pitching looks like it's in good shape and getting better. Lefty Greg Swindell (13–6, 3.37, despite a month on the disabled list) leads a first-rate starting crew that includes RHP Tom Candiotti (13–10, 3.10), LHP Bud Black (12–11, 3.36), and RHP John

Farrell (9–14, 3.63). Rookie LHP Steve Davis (1–1) could get some starts in '90.

The bullpen features super-closer righty Doug Jones (7–10, 32 saves) and ex-Met hero lefty Jesse Orosco (3–4, 2.08). Steve Olin (1–4) and Kevin Wickander should help in '90.

1B Pete O'Brien took his act and his 12 homers to Seattle, leaving the Cleveland infield in the hands of ex-Met All-Pro Keith Hernandez (.233 in only 75 games), up-and-coming leadoff man 2B Jerry Browne (.299, .370 on-base average, 83 runs), SS Felix Fermin (.238, 21 RBIs in 156 games, an all-time major-league low), and 3B Brook Jacoby (.272), along with much-travelled Paul Zuvella (.276).

Without Carter (.243, but 35 homers, 105 RBIs), the outfield relies on pretenders like Cory Snyder (.215, 59 RBIs), ex-Padre Chris James (.243, 65 RBIs), and youngsters like Joey Belle (.225 in 62 games), Dave Hengel, and Beau Allred. The Indians are coming — sometime.

STAT LEADERS — 1989

BATTING
Average: Browne, .299
Runs: Carter, 84
Hits: Browne, 179
Doubles: Carter, 32
Triples: Jacoby, 5
Home Runs: Carter, 35
RBIs: Carter, 105
Stolen Bases: Browne, 14

PITCHING
Wins: Swindell, Candiotti, 13
Losses: Farrell, 14
Complete Games: Farrell, 7
Shutouts: Black, 3
Saves: Jones, 32
Walks: Farrell, 71
Strikeouts: Farrell, 132

AL East
BALTIMORE ORIOLES
1989 Finish: Second
1990 Prediction: Fifth

Joe Orsulak   **Phil Bradley**

The near-miracle Orioles of '89 are history. In 1990 the Birds will sneak up on no one. Do they have the goods to get it done? This probably isn't a championship club, especially with improved clubs like Boston and Cleveland, but the key ingredients are there.

Manager Frank Robinson's young charges picked up much-needed experience in their just-miss pennant chase. The defense remains sound, and the bullpen is good. Now the Birds must put the rest together.

The starting staff begins with lefty Jeff Ballard (18–8, 3.43) and almost ends with righty Bob Milacki (14–12, 3.74). A variety of others, including Brian Holton (5–7) and Pete Harnisch (5–9), couldn't do it. Dave Schmidt (10–13) is off to Montreal. If 1989's No. 1 draft choice, Ben Jefferson, and righty Curt Schilling are ready, the O's have a shot.

The bullpen is keyed by Gregg Olson (5–2, 1.69), whose 27 saves were eight more than all other rookies combined.

All-Pro SS Cal Ripken, Jr., is the glue that holds Robinson's infield together. The lanky Ripken hit only .257 last season, but smacked 21 homers (again) and knocked in 93 runs. He's a real leader. If SS Juan Bell is ready, Ripken could move to 3B. Brother Billy Ripken (.239) should get one last shot at 2B, with Randy Milligan, rookie Francisco Melendez, or a veteran newcomer at first. Craig Worthington (.247) will play somewhere. If surprising Mickey Tettleton's (.258, 26 homers) knee is sound, the O's are set behind the plate.

OF Phil Bradley (.277, 10 triples, 20 steals) arrived in Baltimore in time to key the '89 comeback. Joe Orsulak (.285) was the top Bird hitter. Mike Devereaux (.266) should complete the outfield, though Butch Davis gets a shot in '90.

STAT LEADERS — 1989

BATTING
Average: Bradley, .277
Runs: Bradley, 83
Hits: C. Ripken, 166
Doubles: C. Ripken, 30
Triples: Bradley, 10
Home Runs: Tettleton, 26
RBIs: C. Ripken, 93
Stolen Bases: Devereaux, 22

PITCHING
Wins: Ballard, 18
Losses: Schmidt, 13
Complete Games: Ballard, Johnson, 4
Shutouts: Milacki, 2
Saves: Olson, 27
Walks: Milacki, 88
Strikeouts: Milacki, 113

AL East
NEW YORK YANKEES
1989 Finish: Fifth
1990 Prediction: Sixth

Andy Hawkins

Roberto Kelly

Dallas Green is gone; Bucky Dent is in; Lou Piniella is managing in Cincinnati; and where, oh where, is Billy Martin? Boss Steinbrenner, as quiet as the Yankees' bats for most of '89, will almost certainly be heard from in 1990.

His Yankees don't figure in the AL East race, but with this ball club, you never know. 1B Don Mattingly and 2B Steve Sax form the best right side in the game. Donnie "slumped" to .303, 23 homers, and 113 RBIs in '89, superstar numbers for anyone except him. One-time NL All-Pro Sax crossed leagues and did the same in the AL (.315, .364 on-base average, 88 runs, 205 hits). Not bad. SS Alvaro Espinoza (.282) was a pleasant surprise, but the Yankees haven't had a top 3B since Graig Nettles moved on.

Rookie Brian Dorsett may join C Bob Geren (.288).

A healthy Dave Winfield (missed all of '89 with back surgery) will certainly improve the Yankee OF picture. His recovery remains a major question. Meanwhile, former Blue Jay Jesse Barfield (.234, 23 homers) expects to be in right, alongside impressive Roberto Kelly (.302 and fine defense). Rookie Bernie Williams should get a full shot. Luis Polonia, a defensive horror who finished '89 in the Milwaukee county jail, doesn't figure.

If Dave Righetti (2–6, 3.00, 25 saves) returns to the starting rotation, it will leave the bullpen to Lee Guetterman (5–5, 2.45, 13 saves) and whoever else (ex-Buc Jeff Robinson?) the Boss can find. Andy Hawkins (15–15) and ex-Expo Pascual (Where's the Ballpark?) Perez top the starters, with Clay Parker (4–5), Dave Lapoint (6–9), and possibly lefties Greg Cadaret (5–5) and Chuck Cary (4–4). Righties Kevin Mmahat and Bobby Davidson might fit in here.

STAT LEADERS — 1989

BATTING
Average: Sax, .315
Runs: Sax, 88
Hits: Sax, 205
Doubles: Mattingly, 37
Triples: Polonia, 6
Home Runs: Mattingly, Barfield, 23
RBIs: Mattingly, 113
Stolen Bases: Sax, 43

PITCHING
Wins: Hawkins, 15
Losses: Hawkins, 15
Complete Games: Hawkins, 5
Shutouts: Hawkins, 2
Saves: Righetti, 25
Walks: Hawkins, 76
Strikeouts: Hawkins, 98

AL East
DETROIT TIGERS
1989 Finish: Seventh
1990 Prediction: Seventh

Dave Bergman   **Mike Henneman**

Can you believe it? The Tigers (59–103) had the worst record in the major leagues. They played the kind of baseball that turns managers' hair gray. Of course, that's no problem for their silver-maned boss, Sparky Anderson. This team must be eating the veteran manager alive. There isn't a single department that even the most avid fan can point to with pride.

Let's try to make a case. Aging 2B Lou Whitaker (.251, but 85 RBIs and 28 homers) can still play. His long-time partner, SS Alan Trammell (.243), tries to bounce back from injuries. 1B Dave Bergman is a utility type whose .268 average was the best among all the toothless Tigers last season. Oakland's World Series 2B Tony Phillips arrives as Detroit's 3B, his best position. What about

Rick Schu (.214)? What about Mike Brumley (.198)? What about them? Travis Fryman may be ready to help in '90.

A leading OF light, Gary Pettis (.257), one of the AL's top defensive players, flew the coop to the Rangers and Chet Lemon (.237) has slowed down. But Toronto CF and lead-off man Lloyd Moseby should help.

Catching is in decent shape, with Mike Heath (.263, 10 homers) and Matt Nokes, who should improve on his .250 average but remains a defensive minus. Rookie Phil Clark may be ready to help.

If the starters can deliver the game to the bullpen, the Tigers are okay. Mike Henneman (11-4, 3.70) and Guillermo Hernandez (2-2, 15 saves) can get it done. But holding on long enough is a problem for starters like re-signed Frank Tanana (10-14, 3.58), 39-year-old Doyle Alexander (6-18, 4.44), unhappy Jack Morris (6-14, 4.86), and injury-prone Jeff Robinson (4-5, 4.73). Will Brian Dubois (0-4, but 1.75) and Scott Aldred help? Who knows?

STAT LEADERS — 1989

BATTING
Average: Pettis, .257
Runs: Pettis, Whitaker, 77
Hits: Whitaker, 128
Doubles: Whitaker, 21
Triples: Pettis, 6
Home Runs: Whitaker, 28
RBIs: Whitaker, 85
Stolen Bases: Pettis, 43

PITCHING
Wins: Henneman, 11
Losses: Alexander, 18
Complete Games:
  Morris, 10
Shutouts: Three with 1
Saves: Hernandez, 15
Walks: Alexander, 76
Strikeouts: Tanana, 147

AL West
KANSAS CITY ROYALS
1989 Finish: Second
1990 Prediction: First

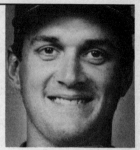

Mark Gubicza   **Kevin Seitzer**

The Royals' 92–70 record (third best in team history) last season was good enough to win the AL East, tie in the NL West, and finish one game behind in the NL East. It was good enough to lose the AL West by seven games. Holy Oakland, Batman!

Who has a one-two pitching punch like the Royals? Imagine facing right-handers Cy Young winner Bret Saberhagen (23–6, 2.16, only 209 hits allowed in 262⅓ innings) and Mark Gubicza (15–11, 3.04) back to back. It's enough to make a right-handed hitter call in sick for a couple of days. Add free agents Storm Davis and Richard Dotson and you've got big trouble. Last year's rookie sensation Tom (Flash) Gordon was 10-2 (3.14) as a reliever, then finished 17–9 (3.64) as a starter. Lefty Charlie Liebrandt (5–11, 5.14) was traded to the Atlanta Braves for switch-hitting 1B Gerald Perry (.252). Young rookies Steve Fireovid, Jose DeJesus, and Bob Buchanan will all be considered for the staff. NL Cy Young winner Mark Davis makes Kaycee's bullpen (Jeff Montgomery, Steve Farr) outstanding.

1B George Brett (.282) remains a premier hitter and a decent defensive player. Hardworking 2B Frank White (.256) can still do it, and 3B Kevin Seitzer (.281) is outstanding. SS Kurt Stillwell (.261) is making the Danny Jackson trade look good for Kaycee. At age 42, C Bob Boone (.274, solid on defense) is a modern-day wonder.

With Willie Wilson (.253, 24 steals), long the Royals' CF, re-signed, Bo (He Sure Knows Baseball) Jackson (.256, 32 homers, 105 RBIs, but 172 strikeouts) stays in LF. Comebacker Jim Eisenreich (.293) can do the job anywhere. Problem child Danny Tartabull may be dealt — if anyone wants him.

STAT LEADERS — 1989

BATTING
Average: Eisenreich, .293
Runs: Jackson, 86
Hits: Seitzer, 168
Doubles: Eisenreich, 33
Triples: Eisenreich, Wilson, 7
Home Runs: Jackson, 32
RBIs: Jackson, 105
Stolen Bases: Eisenreich, 27

*Led league.

PITCHING
Wins: Saberhagen, 23*
Losses: Gubicza, Leibrandt, 11
Complete Games: Saberhagen, 12*
Shutouts: Saberhagen, 4
Saves: Montgomery, Farr, 18
Walks: Gordon, 86
Strikeouts: Saberhagen, 193

AL West
OAKLAND ATHLETICS
1989 Finish: First
1990 Prediction: Second

Dave Henderson   **Mike Moore**

If the re-signed Rickey Henderson plays like Rickey Henderson and if players like Jose Canseco don't self-destruct, the A's have the makings of another dynasty. There isn't a major weakness, but the off-season loss of three major championship players will hurt.

Starting a new decade, manager Tony LaRussa has a lot going for him. Squeaky-voiced righty Dave Stewart (21–9, 3.32) comes off three straight 20-win seasons (and no Cy Young Awards). The rest of the rotation is just about as good, with righties Mike Moore (19–11, 2.61) and Bob Welch (17–8, 3.00). Storm Davis (19–7, 4.36) is gone to Kaycee. Lefty Curt Young (5–9, 3.73) is the No. 4 man, with potential help from rookie lefties Dave Otto and Bryan Clark.

46

If the starters or setup men can get the ball to Dennis Eckersley (4–0, 1.56, a .162 opponents' batting average), you can put the "W" in the book. Eck had more saves (33) than hits allowed (32). Amazing. Backup RHP Todd Burns (6–5, 8 saves) allowed only a .196 opposing batting mark, and lefty Rick Honeycutt (2–2, 2.35) had 12 saves.

The offensive punch is just as impressive. RF Jose Canseco (.269, 17 homers, 57 RBIs in only 65 games) keys an outfield with clutch-hitting CF Dave Henderson (.250) and the $12-million-man, LF Rickey Henderson (.274, 77 stolen bases). Ken Phelps will probably take over as the DH.

The infield is tough, too, with 1B Mark McGwire (.231, but 33 homers and 95 RBIs). Mike Gallego (.252) will move to second for the departed Tony Phillips (Detroit), with a healthy Walt Weiss (.233) at short. 3B Carney Lansford (.336, second in the AL; and 37 steals) and C Terry Steinbach (.273) are All-Pros.

STAT LEADERS — 1989

BATTING
Average: Lansford, .336
Runs: R. Henderson, 113
Hits: Lansford, 185
Doubles: Lansford, 28
Triples: Phillips, 6
Home Runs: McGwire, 33
RBIs: Parker, 97
Stolen Bases: R. Henderson, 77*

PITCHING
Wins: Stewart, 21
Losses: Moore, 11
Complete Games:
   Stewart, 8
Shutouts: Moore, 3
Saves: Eckersley, 33
Walks: Moore, 83
Strikeouts: Moore, 172

*Led league.

AL West
CALIFORNIA ANGELS
1989 Finish: Third
1990 Prediction: Third

Bert Blyleven   **Mark Langston**

Think about it. The California Angels won 91 games last season. Only four major-league clubs won more. Trouble was, two of them — Oakland (99) and Kansas City (92) — played in the Angels' division.

Too bad. Manager Doug Rader did an outstanding job with the talent on hand in Anaheim. He's back in 1990, with a solid corps of starting pitchers including super-star Mark Langston, a fine closer, good defense, and all-around offense. The Angels aren't far away, especially if Oakland doesn't win 99 games again.

Langston joins the Dutch wonder, Bert Blyleven (17–5, 2.73 at age 38), who needs only 29 wins for the magic 300 career victories. He'll make it by age 40. Bert, whose son is a top high school prospect, joins surprising lefty Jim Abbott (12–12, 3.92 in his rookie campaign) and righties Chuck Finley (16–9, 2.57, 156 strikeouts), Kirk McCaskill (15–10, 2.93), and Mike Witt (9–15) to form a top-flight staff. Closer Bryan Harvey (3–3, 25 saves) keys the bullpen with lefty Bob McClure (6–1, 1.55) and righty Greg Minton (4–3, 2.20). Righty Mike Fetters gets a shot.

1B Wally Joyner (.282, 16 homers, 79 RBIs) and 2B Johnny Ray (.289, 62 RBIs) man the right side, though Ray's defense is a problem. SS Dick Schofield (.228) should return from the DL to pair with 3B Jack Howell (a disappointing .228). 2B Bobby Rose and 3B Jeff Manto get a chance this season. C Lance Parrish (.238) is happy to be back in the AL.

The outfield is first-rate. CF Devon White (.245) may be the AL's top defensive outfielder. RF Chili Davis (.271) was the team's top position player. LF Claudell Washington (.273) shocks all of the teams that let him go, and DH Brian Downing (.283) remains a threat.

STAT LEADERS — 1989

BATTING

Average: Ray, .289
Runs: White, 86
Hits; Joyner, 167
Doubles: Joyner, 30
Triples: White, 13
Home Runs: Davis, 22
RBIs: Davis, 90
Stolen Bases: White, 44

PITCHING

Wins: Blyleven, 17
Losses: Witt, 15
Complete Games: Finley, 9
Shutouts: Blyleven, 5*
Saves: Harvey, 25
Walks: Finley, 82
Strikeouts: Finley, 156

*Led league.

AL West
MINNESOTA TWINS
1989 Finish: Fifth
1990 Prediction: Fourth

Brian Harper

Allan Anderson

How do you trade a Cy Young winner? The Twins figured if they couldn't win with Frank Viola, they might as well lose without him. The result: five new arms from the Mets to bolster the Minny staff. Will it pay off in 1990? Probably not.

If the trade works eventually, it will be a plus for the Twins. The club can hit (.276, second in the AL last year), though without much power. The defense isn't bad. Pitching depth is the obvious key.

Only lefty Allan Anderson (17–10, 3.80) and righty Roy Smith (10–6, 3.92) were double-figure winners for the '89 Twins. Anderson is among the AL's best. Some of the old Mets, including righty Rick Aguilera (3–5, but 3.21 with Minnesota) and lefty David West (3–2, but a horrible 6.41 with the Twins), should contribute immediately. Righty Mike Dyer (4–7) may be in the rotation.

Closer Jeff Reardon, the '80s No. 1 reliever, was 5–4 with 31 saves last season; but he's off to Boston, leaving a major hole. The setup men are led by Juan Berenguer (9–3, 3.48).

The left side of the infield features 3B Gary Gaetti (.251, 19 homers in only 130 games) and SS Greg Gagne (.272). It's a great combo. On the right side, hometown favorite 1B Kent Hrbek (.272, 25 homers) should bounce back from an injury-riddled season (109 games). With 2B Wally Backman gone, utility man Al Newman (.253) will get more time at second.

All-World CF Kirby Puckett (AL-leading .339, 45 doubles, 85 RBIs, spectacular defense) makes the outfield great by himself. LF Dan Gladden (.295) gets it done, but RF (Randy Bush?) is a problem area. C Brian Harper can hit (.325), and Tim Laudner (.222) can catch. Neither does both.

STAT LEADERS — 1989

BATTING
Average: Puckett, .339*
Runs: Puckett, 75
Hits: Puckett, 215*
Doubles: Puckett, 45
Triples: Gagne, 7
Home Runs: Hrbek, 25
RBIs: Puckett, 85
Stolen Bases: Newman, 25

PITCHING
Wins: Anderson, 17
Losses: Viola, Rawley, 12
Complete Games: Viola, 7
Shutouts: Viola,
   Anderson, 1
Saves: Reardon, 31
Walks: Rawley, 60
Strikeouts: Viola, 138

*Led league.

AL West
TEXAS RANGERS
1989 Finish: Fourth
1990 Prediction: Fifth

Julio Franco   **Nolan Ryan**

Where do the Texas Rangers go from here? Strong offense, overpowering Nolan Ryan, and shut-the-door Jeff Russell have gotten the ball club over the .500 mark (83–79). How do they go from 83 wins to, say, 93?

It won't be easy. Signing ex-Tiger OF Gary Pettis as a free agent bolsters a so-so defense, a big plus. But that's only part of the puzzle, especially in a division featuring the champion A's and much-improved Angels and Royals.

MVP runner-up Ruben Sierra (.306, 29 homers, 119 RBIs) is the club leader, along with 2B Julio Franco (.316, 66 walks, .386 on-base average). They're great building blocks. 1B Rafael Palmeiro (.275, 64 RBIs) isn't the answer on defense, but he's just about it right now. 2B Fred Manrique (.294) was a pleasant surprise after coming over from Chicago in the Harold Baines deal. SS Jeff Kunkel (.270) continues to improve, and 3B Scott Coolbaugh impressed in a September trial, though rookie 3B Dean Palmer may get the call in '90.

DH Baines (.309, but only .285, three homers, 16 RBIs with Texas) was mildly disappointing. Sierra and Pettis will look to rookie Juan Gonzalez for outfield help this season, though Pete Incaviglia (.236, 21 homers) is a major power authority.

Ageless wonder Ryan, who needs 11 wins for 300, was the AL's toughest starter to hit (.187) last season. At age 42, he struck out 301 in '89, becoming the first AL hurler over age 31 ever to accomplish that feat. He needs help, however. Closer Russell (6–4, 38 saves) will get the "W" when he gets the opportunity. But can re-signed knuckleballer Charlie Hough (10–13, 4.35), Bobby Witt (12–13, 5.14), and young Kevin Brown (12–9, 3.35) get him the ball in time?

STAT LEADERS — 1989

BATTING
Average: Franco, .316
Runs: Baines, 101
Hits: Sierra, 194
Doubles: Sierra, 35
Triples: Sierra, 14*
Home Runs: Sierra, 29
RBIs: Sierra, 119*
Stolen Bases: Espy, 45

*Led league.

PITCHING
Wins: Ryan, 16
Losses: Witt, Hough, 13
Complete Games:
    Brown, 7
Shutouts: Ryan,
    Jeffcoat, 2
Saves: Russell, 38*
Walks: Witt, 114
Strikeouts: Ryan, 301*

AL West
SEATTLE MARINERS
1989 Finish: Sixth
1990 Prediction: Sixth

Ken Griffey, Jr.

Alvin Davis

The "Under New Ownership" sign that's hanging outside the Seattle Kingdome is welcome news to Mariners' fans. Under former owner George Argyros, the M's suffered through lean years (putting it kindly), with some unbelievable on- and off-field decisions.

With the leadership of manager Jim Lefebvre, Seattle is playing better than their sixth-place record indicates. That may translate into a better finish in 1990.

The M's major weakness is starting pitching. (Imagine this club with Mark Langston and Mike Moore!) But there are some bright spots, including righty Scott Bankhead (14–6, 3.34), young Erik Hanson (9–5, 3.18), Brian Holman (8–10, 3.44), and basketball-sized (6'10") Randy Johnson

(7–9). Middle relief is in bigger trouble, though Billy Swift (7–3, 4.43) impressed a few folks. Rookie RHP Julio Solano may help out. Closer Mike Schooler may rise in AL ranks after his 2.81 ERA and 33 saves (despite a 1–7 record).

Lefebvre will continue to build his offense around new DH Alvin Davis (.305, 21 homers, 95 RBIs). Amazingly, Davis hit .365 in Seattle, .265 on the road. Strange. Ex-Indian Pete O'Brien takes Davis's spot at 1B. 2B Harold Reynolds (.300) is one of the AL's best, but 3B Jim Presley (.236, only 12 homers) may be in trouble. SS Omar Vizquel (.220) should improve on his rookie stats.

Youth will be served in the outfield, where young vet Henry Cotto (.264) does well defensively in CF. Ken Griffey, Jr. (.264, 16 homers), debuted well, along with Greg Briley (.266, 13 homers). Sometime trouble-maker Jeffrey Leonard (.254, 24 homers, 93 RBIs) will DH — if he wants to. Scott Bradley (.274) and Dave Valle (.237) should again platoon behind the plate.

STAT LEADERS — 1989

BATTING
Average: Davis, .305
Runs: Reynolds, 87
Hits: Reynolds, 184
Doubles: Davis, 30
Triples: Reynolds, 9
Home Runs: Leonard, 24
RBIs: Davis, 95
Stolen Bases: Reynolds, 25

PITCHING
Wins: Bankhead, 14
Losses: Holman, 10
Complete Games: Holman, 6
Shutouts: Bankhead,
 Holman, 2
Saves: Schooler, 33
Walks: Johnson, 70
Strikeouts: Bankhead, 140

CHICAGO WHITE SOX
1989 Finish: Seventh
1990 Prediction: Seventh

Ozzie Guillen

Carlton Fisk

White Sox manager Jeff Torborg is one of the world's greatest optimists. Good thing. The Sox, who finished 29½ games off the AL West pace last season, don't have much to cheer about. Even worse, while several AL West clubs spent the off-season getting stronger, the White Sox stood still.

There's some hope, of course. The infield isn't bad, closer Bobby Thigpen will lead the bullpen (if he isn't traded), and the team can hit. Otherwise, there isn't much.

Start with the infield. With ex-Ranger Scott Fletcher (.253) at second, exciting Ozzie Guillen (.253) at short, and hot prospect Robin Ventura, a U.S. Olympic veteran, at third, there are possibilities. 1B Greg Walker (.210) still hasn't recovered from the seizures that almost killed him in '88.

He also had shoulder surgery in the off-season. Ex-Dodger Tracy Woodson (obtained for P Jeff Bittiger) might blossom in Chicago.

The outfield isn't nearly as solid. Ivan Calderon (.286, 87 RBIs) hit 14 homers, which, unbelievably, led the team. The rest of the crew, including flaky Darryl Boston (.252), Dave Gallagher (.266), and Lance Johnson (.300 in 50 games), doesn't excite. Aged (he's 42) C Carlton Fisk (.293, 13 homers) continues to amaze, though Ron Karkovice (.264) is ready to go.

Righties Jeff McDowell and Wilson Alvarez will try to shore up Chicago's pitching. Righties Melido Perez (11–14, 5.01) and Shawn Hillegas (7–11, 4.74) join lefties Steve Rosenberg (4–13) and Greg Hibbard (6–7, 3.21) as the Sox try to turn their mound staff around. The loss of RHP Richard Dotson (5–12) to Kansas City doesn't help. RHP Thigpen (2–6, 34 saves) is one of the AL's best. If he's dealt, the Sox won't even know how to spell *relief*.

STAT LEADERS — 1989

BATTING
Average: Calderon, .289
Runs: Calderon, 83
Hits: Calderon, 178
Doubles: Calderon, 34
Triples: Calderon, 9
Home Runs: Calderon, 14
RBIs: Calderon, 87
Stolen Bases: Guillen, 36

PITCHING
Wins: Perez, 11
Losses: Perez, 14
Complete Games:
   Four with 2
Shutouts: King, 1
Saves: Thigpen, 34
Walks: Perez, 90
Strikeouts: Perez, 141

Does he or doesn't he (load up the ball, that is)? Houston's Mike Scott doesn't care what you think; he just wins, baby!

National League
TEAM PREVIEWS

NL East
NEW YORK METS
1989 Finish: Second
1990 Prediction: First

Sid Fernandez

Dave Magadan

The surprise team of 1989? No doubt about it — the New York Mets. Expected to run away and hide from the NL East, the Metsies never put it together and barely got up to finish second, six games behind the upstart Cubs.

The picture for 1990 isn't pretty, though it's far from ugly. Manager Davey Johnson is back, which surprised a few folks, including Johnson himself. A couple of his coaches are gone, a bunch of his veterans are gone; and if the Mets get off to a rocky start, he may be gone, too.

Barring some deals — the Mets don't generally go for free agents — Dave Magadan (.286, no power) will open at 1B, where Keith Hernandez was sent packing. Gregg Jefferies (.258, 56 RBIs, after a poor start) will return at second and may hit in May and June the way he did last August and September. Defensive whiz Kevin Elster (.231) should be back at SS, with All-Pro Howard Johnson (.287, 36 homers, 101 RBIs, 41 steals) at third. Or manager Johnson might juggle this whole group.

RF Darryl Strawberry is back after a year off, not just an off-year (.225, 29 homers, 77 RBIs). It will shock a few folks if Juan Samuel (.235, 42 steals, 120 strikeouts) is the CF, but Kevin McReynolds (.272, 85 RBIs) will be in LF if he's in New York. Barry Lyons (.247) is the No. 1 catcher, with Gary Carter gone.

Starting pitching remains the Mets' top asset. Can you top Dwight Gooden (9–4, despite missing two months), Frank Viola (5–5 with the Mets), Sid Fernandez (14–5, 2.83), David Cone (14–8), and either Bob Ojeda (13–11) or Ron Darling (14–14)? If ex-Red John Franco is more consistent than Randy Myers, the bullpen is solid, though a righty closer would really help.

STAT LEADERS — 1989

BATTING
Average: Johnson, .287
Runs: Johnson, 104*
Hits: Johnson, 164
Doubles: Johnson, 41
Triples: Three with 3
Home Runs: Johnson, 36
RBIs: Johnson, 101
Stolen Bases: Samuel, 42

*Tied for league lead.

PITCHING
Wins: Fernandez, Cone, Darling, 14
Losses: Darling, 14
Complete Games: Fernandez, 6
Shutouts: Three with 2
Saves: Myers, 24
Walks: Ojeda, 78
Strikeouts: Fernandez, 198

ST. LOUIS CARDINALS
1989 Finish: Third
1990 Prediction: Second

Jose DeLeon   **Pedro Guerrero**

A few seasons back, longtime Cardinal owner Gussie Busch offered manager Whitey Herzog a lifetime contract. The White Rat looked at the 85-year-old Busch and asked, "Your lifetime or mine?" Busch died last year, and Whitey is back, finally settling that question. Whitey will be back for as long as he'd like to be.

There's plenty for Whitey to like. A starting pitcher or two (easier written than done) and a little power is about all he needs for another NL East title. The Cards have speed and defense to burn.

If LHP Greg Matthews and/or RHP Danny Cox (elbow) returns healthy, Herzog's problems may be solved. Joe Magrane (18–9, 2.91) zoomed back from a 5–9 '88 season, and Jose DeLeon (16–12) is usually on target. Ex-Expo

Bryn Smith (10–11) should help. Ken Hill (7–15) is better than his record (lost nine of last 10). Todd Worrell (3–5, 20 saves), after surgery, figures to miss a couple of months, but Frank DiPino (9–0, 2.45) was '89's biggest surprise. Ken Dayley (4–3, 12 saves) is a solid bullpen contributor.

1B Pedro Guerrero needs help. The ex-Dodger hit .311 with 42 doubles and 117 RBIs last year, and represented most of the Cardinal offense. A healthy Willie McGee (.236) in CF would help enormously, as would a renewed Vincent Coleman (.254, a league-leading 65 steals) in LF. RF Tom Brunansky (.239, 85 RBIs, 20 HRs) must up his power game. OF Milt Thompson (.290, 68 RBIs) came up big last season.

The left side of the infield is solid, with aging but reliable Ozzie Smith (.273, 29 steals) at SS and Terry Pendleton (.264) at 3B. Young Todd Zeile (.256) replaces departed Tony Pena (.259) behind the plate.

STAT LEADERS — 1989

BATTING
Average: Guerrero, .311
Runs: Coleman, 94
Hits: Guerrero, 177
Doubles: Guerrero, 42**
Triples: Coleman, 9
Home Runs: Brunansky, 20
RBIs: Guerrero, 117
Stolen Bases: Coleman, 65*

PITCHING
Wins: Magrane, 18
Losses: Hill, 15
Complete Games:
  Magrane, 9
Shutouts: Magrane,
  DeLeon, 3
Saves: Worrell, 20
Walks: Hill, 99
Strikeouts: DeLeon, 201*

*Led league.
**Tied for league lead.

NL East
CHICAGO CUBS

1989 Finish: First
1990 Prediction: Third

Mark Grace   **Greg Maddux**

And the wait continues. Chicago Cub fans haven't seen their team in a World Series since Harry Truman was President (1945). Good news: The Cubs have the people in place to make it while George Bush is in the White House.

The Cubbies shocked more than a few folks, maybe even manager Don Zimmer, by clawing their way to the NL East title in '89. They did it mainly with young talent, three solid starters, and amazing relief work.

The big three arms are back, led by old reliable Rick Sutcliffe (16–11), Greg Maddux (19–12), and surprising ex-Pirate Mike Bielecki (18–7). Scott Sanderson (11–9) was a free agent who insisted on remaining a starter. He signed a contract with Oakland. The return of injured RHP Mike Harkey would help enormously.

Ex-Ranger Mitch Williams (4–4, 36 saves) should continue to finish every game that Les Lancaster (4–2, 1.36, 8 saves) doesn't.

The right side of the infield is in superb shape. 1B Mark Grace (.314, 79 RBIs) would be an all-leaguer in any league without Will Clark. 2B Ryne Sandberg (.290, 30 homers) is the NL's best. On the left side, SS Shawon Dunston (.278) has improved offensively and has a gun for an arm. If former Olympian Ty Griffin makes it at 3B, it will be a plus.

The NL's top two rookies in '89, OFs Jerome Walton (.293) and Dwight Smith (.324), will rejoin super slugger RF Andre Dawson (.252, 21 homers), unless Smith is dealt for pitching help. There is depth behind the plate if Damon Berryhill (.257) returns healthy to join Rick Wrona (.283) or Joe Girardi (.248).

The Cubs should be in the fight again.

STAT LEADERS — 1989

BATTING

Average: Grace, .314
Runs: Sandberg, 104*
Hits: Sandberg, 176
Doubles: Grace, 28
Triples: Three with 6
Home Runs: Sandberg, 30
RBIs: Grace, 79
Stolen Bases: Walton, 24

PITCHING

Wins: Maddux, 19
Losses: Maddux, 12
Complete Games:
    Maddux, 7
Shutouts: Bielecki, 3
Saves: Williams, 36
Walks: Maddux, 82
Strikeouts: Sutcliffe, 153

*Tied for league lead.

NL East
PITTSBURGH PIRATES
1989 Finish: Fifth
1990 Prediction: Fourth

John Smiley   **Bobby Bonilla**

A year ago, the Bucs were a second-place team with a brilliant future. Now the Pirates are a confused fifth-place team, with an eye cast over their shoulder at the last-place Phillies instead of the four clubs ahead of them. In fairness, the Pirates had more than their share of injuries in '89, but even the healthy players didn't do much.

To be sure, Pittsburgh has a few guys that anyone would love to have. Bobby Bonilla (.281, 24 homers, 86 RBIs), an embarrassment at third base, will return to the outfield, probably in right. He should be more comfortable. If Bobby Bonds is back (.248), he should be in LF, with Andy Van Slyke (a horrible .237, only 53 RBIs) looking to bounce back in CF.

Sid Bream (.222) is back at 1B, with Jose

Lind (.232) trying to come back at 2B. Young Jay Bell (.258) figures to be the Pirate SS for a while, and Jeff King (.195) may get a full shot at 3B unless the Bucs trade for a proven third sacker.

The Bucs obtained C Don Slaught (.251) from the Yanks to platoon with Mike LaValliere (.316, despite missing three months with knee surgery last season). Dann Bilardello (.225) and Junior Ortiz (.217) can't do it.

RHP Doug Drabek (14–12, 2.80 ERA) and LHP John Smiley (12–8, 2.81) are the keys to a battling pitching staff. Bob Walk (13–10, 4.41) can get the job done. Manager Jim Leyland will have to find a solid fourth starter before he can worry about a fifth.

Though Jim Gott, who pitched only two thirds of an inning last season, signed with Los Angeles, the Bucs' bullpen, one of the few strengths in '89, will be stronger. Bill Landrum (2–3, 26 saves) filled in admirably last year.

STAT LEADERS — 1989

BATTING
Average: Bonilla, .281
Runs: Bonds, Bonilla, 96
Hits: Bonilla, 173
Doubles: Bonilla, 37
Triples: Bonilla, 10
Home Runs: Bonilla, 24
RBIs: Bonilla, 86
Stolen Bases: Bonds, 32

PITCHING
Wins: Drabek, 14
Losses: Robinson, 13
Complete Games: Drabek, Smiley, 8
Shutouts: Drabek, 5
Saves: Landrum, 26
Walks: Drabek, 69
Strikeouts: Drabek, Smiley, 123

NL East
PHILADELPHIA PHILLIES
1989 Finish: Sixth
1990 Prediction: Fifth

Lenny Dykstra   **Roger McDowell**

Manager Nick Leyva, a longtime Cardinal coach, did such a good job in leading the Philadelphia Phillies to a last-place 67–95 record last year that he'll be given another shot at it in 1990. Hang in there, Nick. It will get better.

The Phillies' recovery, however, will take time. Lots of it. Starting pitching is in terrible shape. Rookie Pat Combs went 4–0 with a 2.09 ERA in September and earned a berth for '90, joining solid citizen Ken Howell (12–12, 3.44, 164 strikeouts). Some promising young folks are on their way, including Dennis Cook (7–8, 3.72), Terry Mulholland (4–7, 4.92), Jason Grimsley (1–3), and a rebounding Bruce Ruffin (6–10). The bullpen figures to be one of the NL's best, featuring ex-Expo Jeff Parrett (12–6, 2.98, 6 saves) and ex-Met Roger McDowell (4–8, 1.96, 23 saves), who rebounded in Philly. The pen has to deal with fewer hopeless causes.

The Philadelphia front office spent the off-season pursuing talented starters, a catcher, and right-handed hitting, in general. Trouble was, the club didn't have much talent to offer.

The outfield figures to be in good shape, with Lenny Dykstra (.237, 30 steals, only .222 with Philadelphia) re-signed in center and Von Hayes (.259, 26 homers, 78 RBIs) in right. Rookie Ron Jones (.290 in a late trial) could start in left, unless Hayes is dealt. Leyva will have to find a spot for John Kruk's bat. Kruk (.187 when he came to Philly last June 3) finished at .300.

1B Ricky Jordan rallied to hit .285 with 75 RBIs in '89 and is a future star. SS Dickie Thon (.271) continues his big-time comeback. Steve Jeltz (.243) and Charley Hayes (.257) will get plenty of action. C Darren Daulton (.201) continues to struggle. The Phillies also re-signed C Steve Lake.

STAT LEADERS — 1989

BATTING
Average: Herr, .287
Runs: V. Hayes, 93
Hits: Herr, 161
Doubles: Dykstra, 32
Triples: Kruk, Herr, 6
Home Runs: Hayes, 26
RBIs: Hayes, 78
Stolen Bases: Dykstra, 30

PITCHING
Wins: Howell, Parrett, 12
Losses: Carman, 15
Complete Games:
   Four with 2
Shutouts: Six with 1
Saves: McDowell, 23
Walks: Howell, Carman, 86
Strikeouts: Howell, 164

NL East
MONTREAL EXPOS
1989 Finish: Fourth
1990 Prediction: Sixth

Tim Wallach   **Andres Galarraga**

Is it time for the Expos to rebuild again? Montreal dealt a bunch of talent to Seattle for Mark Langston last summer. The purpose: Buy the 1989 NL East championship. The plan failed, the Expos finished fourth, and Langston moved on to the Angels. The NL East cellar could be the next stop.

Now manager Buck Rodgers and GM Dave Dombrowski must make major decisions. Pitching, always an Expo strength, is a potential problem. Pascual Perez (9–13) signed with the Yanks, and Bryn Smith (10–11) signed with the Cards. Dennis Martinez (16–7, 3.18) will be the kingpin. If ex-Red Sox Oil Can Boyd gets his act together, he'll be a big hero in Canada. A healthy Joe Hesketh (6–4) would help, and rookie righty Mark Gardner (0–3) must get it done now.

The bullpen is Tim Burke (9–3, 28 saves) and little else.

Andres Galarraga must come back from a .257 (but 23 homers, 85 RBIs) season at 1B. Is rookie Delino DeShields ready to take over at 2B for departing Damaso Garcia? Tim Wallach (.277, 13 homers) was the 'Spos MVP in '89 and could repeat. Spike Owen (.233) is the shortstop — for now. The club picked up Tom Foley's option for 1990.

LF Tim Raines (a disappointing .286, 41 steals) remains a solid threat, but was rumored on the trading block during the winter. Rookie Larry Walker could take over in RF if Hubie Brooks (.268) leaves. Walker could be joined by Marquis Grissom, a candidate for the CF job, too.

Catching is in decent shape with Nelson Santovenia (.250) and Mike Fitzgerald (.238).

Can Montreal win with youngsters like DeShields, Grissom, Walker, and Gardner in the regular lineup? The Cubs did it in 1989, but that formula doesn't always work.

STAT LEADERS — 1989

BATTING
Average: Raines, .286
Runs: Three with 76
Hits: Wallach, 159
Doubles: Wallach, 42*
Triples: Da. Martinez, 9
Home Runs: Galarraga, 23
RBIs: Galarraga, 85
Stolen Bases: Raines, 41

PITCHING
Wins: De. Martinez, 16
Losses: Perez, 13
Complete Games:
  Langston, 6
Shutouts: Langston, 4
Saves: Burke, 28
Walks: Langston, 93
Strikeouts: Langston, 175

*Tied for league lead.

NL West
SAN DIEGO PADRES
1989 Finish: Second
1990 Finish: First

Bruce Hurst   **Joe Carter**

After finishing a flying second in '89, the Padres enter the new decade with enormous optimism. Though free-agent, Cy Young winner Mark Davis, possibly baseball's best closer, left for Kansas City, that optimism remains high. Trader Jack McKeon has the makings of a championship ball club on hand.

The top half of the lineup borders on awesome. 2B Roberto Alomar (.295, .347 on-base average) will lead off, with All-Pro RF Tony Gwynn batting second. Gwynn is the type of hitter you pay to watch. His .336 mark earned him another NL bat crown last season. The new man in town, ex-Indian CF Joe Carter (35 homers, 105 RBIs) hits third. And 1B Jack Clark (.242, 26 homers, 94 RBIs) can power any ball club. He could move to the outfield if the Padres pick up a veteran 1B.

C Benito Santiago will bat fifth, feeling much more secure now that Sandy Alomar, Jr., is off to Cleveland. Outfielders Chris James and Carmelo Martinez are both gone, and OF Fred Lynn (.241) was signed as a free agent. Mike Pagliarulo (.196) could provide some punch at 3B. SS Garry Templeton was re-signed for '90 and '91. He remains a hard worker at age 33.

There's good depth in the starting rotation, thanks to the fine rookie performance of RHP Andy Benes (6–3, 3.51) and the comeback by RHP Eric Show (8–6). RHP Ed Whitson (16–11, 2.66) and LHP Bruce Hurst (15–11, 2.69) are solid. LHP Dennis Rasmussen (10–10, 4.26) could be packed off elsewhere. Ex-Giant Craig Lefferts (20 saves) replaces Davis.

The A's exposed the Giants and their aging pitching staff during the World Series. The Padres are ready to swoop in.

STAT LEADERS — 1989

BATTING

Average: Gwynn, .336*
Runs: Gwynn, R. Alomar, 82
Hits: Gwynn, 203*
Doubles: Gwynn, R. Alomar, 27
Triples: Roberts, 8
Home Runs: Clark, 26
RBIs: Clark, 94
Stolen Bases: R. Alomar, 42

PITCHING

Wins: Whitson, 16
Losses: Terrell, 13
Complete Games:
    Hurst, 10**
Shutouts: Hurst, 2
Saves: Davis, 44*
Walks: Rasmussen, 72
Strikeouts: Hurst, 179

*Led league.
**Tied for league lead.

NL West
SAN FRANCISCO GIANTS
1989 Finish: First
1990 Prediction: Second

Scott Garrelts   **Robby Thompson**

The Giants, who survived a variety of
injuries to their pitchers, a late-season
charge by the San Diego Padres, the fired-
up Chicago Cubs, even an earthquake,
were dismantled by the Oakland A's in the
World Series. Whether they can bounce back
from that rout is the key to their 1990 season.

The ability is there. The Jints have a great
offensive lineup, keyed by the top five: CF
Brett Butler (.283, 59 walks, 31 steals), an
outstanding defensive player, is a pest at
the plate and on the bases. 2B Robby
Thompson (.241) sets up the NL's best one-
two punch, 1B Will Clark (.333, 23 homers,
111 RBIs) and LF Kevin Mitchell (.291, 47
homers, 125 RBIs). 3B Matt Williams (.202,
18 homers in limited action) adds another
dose of power.

Ex-Astro Kevin Bass (.300) should solve the RF problems. (Candy Maldonado and Pat Sheridan are gone.) SS Jose Uribe (.221) provides a great glove but no offensive punch. There's plenty of depth all over the field, led by youngsters like Greg Litton and Ernest Riles, who'll get a good look in 1990. C Terry Kennedy, expected to return, leads the catching corps.

Unless the Giants make a move or two, pitching is a disaster waiting to happen. Whether it happens in '90 is another question. Ex-reliever RHP Scottie Garrelts (14–5) should do it again, but tubby Rick Reuschel (17–8) will be 41 in May, Bob Knepper was 7–12, Mike LaCoss (10–10) was inconsistent, and Don Robinson (12–11) has been injury-prone. Dave Dravecky, after cancer treatment, has retired.

If the starters can get the ball to Steve Bedrosian (23 saves) (free-agent Craig Lefferts moved to San Diego), they'll be okay.

STAT LEADERS — 1989

BATTING
Average: Clark, .333
Runs: Clark, 104**
Hits: Clark, 196
Doubles: Clark, 38
Triples: Thompson, 11*
Home Runs: Mitchell, 47*
RBIs: Mitchell, 125*
Stolen Bases: Butler, 31

PITCHING
Wins: Reuschel, 17
Losses: Knepper, 12
Complete Games:
  Robinson, 5
Shutouts: Three with 1
Saves: Bedrosian, 23
Walks: Knepper, 75
Strikeouts: Garrelts, 119

*Led league.
**Tied for league lead.

NL West
CINCINNATI REDS
1989 Finish: Fifth
1990 Prediction: Third

Tom Browning   **Paul O'Neill**

Team Turmoil should bounce back from
the 1989 Pete Rose fiasco. There's too much
talent here for a fifth-place team, and new
manager Lou Piniella might just put it all
together. Well, maybe he'll put most of it
together.

Unless the Reds deal Eric Davis, the out-
field is fairly solid. They don't get much
better than CF Davis (.281, 34 homers, 101
RBIs), when he has his act together. RF Paul
O'Neill (.276, 15 homers, 74 RBIs) is first-rate.
They need a right-handed bat in left where
Ken Griffey, Sr., is 40 years old. OF Rolando
Roomes (.263) struck out 100 times in 315 at-
bats last season.

SS Barry Larkin (.342 in a half season in
'89) is an All-Pro and leads the Reds' infield.
1B Todd Benzinger (.245) and 3B Chris Sabo

(.260) need to provide much more punch for Cincy to move up. The Reds also need a premier 2B, where Ron Oester (.246) isn't the answer. Bo Diaz is probably gone because young Joe Oliver (.272) looks like a fine everyday backstop.

Pitching will be a challenge for Piniella. The makings are there. If LHP Danny Jackson (6–11) and Jose Rijo (7–6) bounce back, they'll be on their way. Tom Browning (15–12) and young Scott Scudder (4–9) should complete a decent rotation. Tim Leary (8–14) is gone to the Yankees, but Norm Charlton (8–3) and Jack Armstrong (2–3) offer interesting possibilities.

John Franco (32 saves), just so-so in late '89, goes to the Mets for flaky, hard-throwing Randy Myers. Myers joins another flake, Rob Dibble (10–5, 2.09), to form the core of a solid bullpen.

If the problems and the injuries of the recent past are behind them, the Reds could get back into the hunt quickly.

STAT LEADERS — 1989

BATTING
Average: Davis, .281
Runs: Davis, 74
Hits: Benzinger, 154
Doubles: Benzinger, 28
Triples: Larkin, Quinones, 4
Home Runs: Davis, 34
RBIs: Davis, 101
Stolen Bases: Davis, 21

PITCHING
Wins; Browning, 15
Losses: Leary, 14
Complete Games:
  Browning, 9
Shutouts: Browning,
  Mahler, 2
Saves: Franco, 32
Walks: Leary, 68
Strikeouts: Dibble, 141

LOS ANGELES DODGERS

1989 Finish: Fourth
1990 Prediction: Fourth

Jay Howell

Tim Belcher

The Dodgers deflected a lot of criticism of their 1989 performance by spending the summer talking about manager Tommy Lasorda's diet. You wonder whether Tommy would swap the pounds for a few runs. The Dodgers were toothless in '89.

Start with pitching, because that's the Dodgers' story. Without much support, '88 Cy Young winner Orel Hershiser slumped to 15–15 despite a 2.31 ERA. In fact, though the Dodgers finished six games under .500 for the season, the pitching staff's ERA was a marvelous 2.95. Righty Tim Belcher was 15–12 with a 2.82 ERA. Youngsters John Wetteland (5–8) and Ramon Martinez (6–4) are ready to contribute. Fernando Valenzuela (10–13, 3.43) bounced back late and could help if he's OK. The Dodgers dealt

Tracy Woodson to the White Sox for Jeff Bittiger. Ex-Pirate Jim Gott fits in well.

The bullpen is in capable hands. Jay Howell (5–3, 1.58, a franchise-record 28 saves) is one of the NL's best. Alejandro Pena (4–3, 2.13) is a premier setup man. There's plenty of depth here, too.

Offense is another story. There wasn't any last year. 1B Eddie Murray, the infield's weak defensive link, was the lone offensive spark, with a .247 average, but 20 homers and 88 RBIs. Ex-Yankee captain Willie Randolph (.282) did all that was expected of him. 3B Jeff Hamilton (.245) needs to provide more punch. SS Alfredo Griffin (.247) has lost a step, as has C Mike Scioscia (.250).

CF John Shelby (.183) is done as a Dodger. With healthy knees, World Series hero Kirk Gibson (.213) and ex-Red Kal Daniels (.246) could make major contributions, though they both play left field and there's no DH in the NL.

STAT LEADERS — 1989

BATTING
Average: Randolph, .282
Runs: Murray, 66
Hits; Randolph, 155
Doubles: Hamilton, 35
Triples: Four with 2
Home Runs: Murray, 20
RBIs: Murray, 88
Stolen Bases: Harris, 14

*Led league.

PITCHING
Wins: Hershiser,
   Belcher, 15
Losses: Hershiser, 15
Complete Games:
   Belcher, 10*
Shutouts: Belcher, 8*
Saves: Howell, 28
Walks: Valenzuela, 98
Strikeouts: Belcher, 200

NL West
HOUSTON ASTROS
1989 Finish: Third
1990 Prediction: Fifth

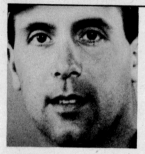

Jim Deshaies   **Glenn Davis**

The Houston Astros lost the whole NL West shooting match by only six games last summer. Where would they have been if they hadn't allowed Nolan Ryan to bolt to the Rangers?

Spilled milk, of course. Forget it. No pitcher can provide the power that the 'Stros so desperately need. Only 1B Glenn Davis (.269, 34 homers) provided any last year. The loss of free-agent Kevin Bass (.300, 44 RBIs) to San Francisco doesn't help. Young Eric Anthony, an early rookie-of-the-year candidate, could open in left and should hit with power. Glenn Wilson (.266) will be in right, after a whirlwind tour of both leagues.

2B Bill Doran will try to bounce back from a strange '89. He hit only .219, 53 points below his career average, and only .131 after the All-Star break. Weird! 3B Ken Caminiti (.255) and SS Rafael Ramirez (.246), if he signs, are strong on the left side. If Ramirez goes, untested Eric Yelding owns the position.

Catching, a Houston weakness since oil prices were skyrocketing, is now in the capable hands of Craig Biggio (.257).

Three quarters of a starting staff are in place. The Cy Young runner-up, righty Mike Scott (20–10, 3.10), is one of the NL's best. He's joined by RHP Mark Portugal (7–1, 2.75) and LHP Jim Deshaies (15–10, 2.91). Portugal has been around without much success and isn't a sure bet yet. The fourth starter remains a question mark. Jim Clancy (7–14) didn't get it done in '89, but lefty Darryl Kile is coming on quickly. If Bill Gullickson can come back after a year in Japan, he'll help.

The bullpen starts with veteran RHP Dave Smith (3–4, 25 saves), with Danny Darwin (11–4, 2.36, 7 saves) and Larry Andersen (4–4, 1.54) as setup men.

STAT LEADERS — 1989

BATTING
Average: Davis, .269
Runs: Davis, 87
Hits: Davis, 156
Doubles: Caminiti, 31
Triples: Three with 4
Home Runs: Davis, 34
RBIs: Davis, 89
Stolen Bases: Young, 34

PITCHING
Wins: Scott, 20*
Losses: Clancy, 14
Complete Games: Scott, 9
Shutouts: Deshaies, 3
Saves: Smith, 25
Walks, Deshaies, 79
Strikeouts: Scott, 172

*Led league.

NL West
ATLANTA BRAVES
1989 Finish: Sixth
1990 Prediction: Sixth

Lonnie Smith

Tom Glavine

You're the Atlanta Braves' general manager. You've got a few good players, a few aging veterans, some young "future" talent. You've been at the bottom of the NL West since sometime after the end of the Civil War. Where do you go from here?

The answers aren't easy. As long as owner Ted Turner has a decent balance in his checking account, you can think about free agents. That's how 1B Nick Esasky (.277, 30 homers, 108 RBIs) arrived from Boston, which freed Atlanta to move Gerald Perry to Kansas City for LHP Charlie Liebrandt.

There are some relatively happy infield decisions to make, involving SS Andres Thomas (.213) and SS-3B Jeff Blauser (.270). Blauser will play somewhere. Oddibe McDowell or Ron Gant (only .177) will probably end up in CF, alongside Atlanta's entire 1989 offense, comebacker Lonnie Smith (.315, 21 homers, 79 RBIs, 25 steals). Does RF Dale Murphy (.228, 20 homers, 84 RBIs) have another season left? Look for 1B Drew Denson, 2B Mark Lemke, and 3B Ed Whited to get a full look this spring.

There are plenty of young catchers in the Braves' organization. Either Kelly Mann or Francisco Cabrera could get the call this season. It's a weak area now, though there's plenty of fine talent on the way.

Pitching is in much better shape. RHP John Smoltz (12–11) and LHP Tom Glavine (14–8) are as close to untouchable as anyone Atlanta has. LHP Derek Lilliquist (8–10) and RHP Pete Smith (5–14) will start, if they aren't dealt. Gary Eave, Tommy Greene, and Kent Mercker provide tremendous depth. LHP Mike Stanton (0–1, 7 saves) looks like the '90 closer.

With little power, no run production, poor catching, and shoddy defense, the Braves have a long way to go.

STAT LEADERS — 1989

BATTING
Average: L. Smith, .315
Runs: L. Smith, 89
Hits: L. Smith, 152
Doubles: L. Smith, 34
Triples: L. Smith, McDowell, 4
Home Runs: L. Smith, 21
RBIs: Murphy, 84
Stolen Bases: L. Smith, 25

PITCHING
Wins: Glavine, 14
Losses: P. Smith, 14
Complete Games:
  Glavine, 6
Shutouts: Glavine, 4
Saves: Boever, 21
Walks: Smoltz, 72
Strikeouts: Smoltz, 168

Ol' Man (Nolan) Ryan just keeps rolling along; the all-time "K" leader is just 11 wins short of the magic 300-win circle.

1989
STATISTICS

AMERICAN LEAGUE
Batting

(25 or more at-bats)
*Bats Left-Handed   †Switch-Hitter

Batter and Club	AVG	G	AB	R	H	HR	RBI	SB
Aguayo, L., Cle.	.175	47	97	7	17	1	8	0
Allanson, A., Cle.	.232	111	323	30	75	3	17	4
Anderson, B., Bal.*	.207	94	266	44	55	4	16	16
Anderson, K., Cal.	.229	86	223	27	51	0	17	1
Armas, T., Cal.	.257	60	202	22	52	11	30	0
Backman, W., Min.†	.231	87	299	33	69	1	26	1
Baines, H., Chi.-Tex.*	.309	146	505	73	156	16	72	0
Baker, D., Min.†	.295	43	78	17	23	0	9	0
Balboni, S., N.Y.	.237	110	300	33	71	17	59	0
Barfield, J., Tor.-N.Y.	.234	150	521	79	122	23	67	5
Barrett, M., Bos.	.256	86	336	31	86	1	27	4
Beane, B., Oak.	.241	37	79	8	19	0	11	3
Bell, B., Tex.	.183	34	82	4	15	0	3	0
Bell, G., Tor.	.297	153	613	88	182	18	104	4
Belle, J., Cle.	.225	62	218	22	49	7	37	2
Bergman, D., Det.*	.268	137	385	38	103	7	37	1
Bichette, D., Cal.	.210	48	138	13	29	3	15	3
Blankenship, L., Oak.	.232	58	125	22	29	1	4	5
Blowers, M., N.Y.	.263	13	38	2	10	0	3	0
Boggs, W., Bos.*	.330	156	621	113	205	3	54	2
Boone, B., K.C.	.274	131	405	33	111	1	43	3
Borders, P., Tor.	.257	94	241	22	62	3	29	2
Bosley, T., Tex.*	.225	37	40	5	9	1	9	2
Boston, D., Chi.*	.252	101	218	34	55	5	23	7
Bradley, P., Bal.	.277	144	545	83	151	11	55	20
Bradley, S., Sea.*	.274	103	270	21	74	3	37	1
Braggs, G., Mil.	.247	144	514	77	127	15	66	17
Brantley, M., Sea.	.157	34	108	14	17	0	8	2
Brenly, B., Tor.	.170	48	88	9	15	1	6	1
Brett, G., K.C.*	.282	124	457	67	129	12	80	14
Briley, G., Sea.*	.266	115	394	52	105	13	52	11

Batter and Club	AVG	G	AB	R	H	HR	RBI	SB
Brock, G., Mil.*	.265	107	373	40	99	12	52	6
Brookens, T., N.Y.	.226	66	168	14	38	4	14	1
Brower, B., N.Y.	.232	26	69	9	16	2	3	3
Brown, C., Det.	.193	17	57	3	11	0	4	0
Browne, J., Cle.†	.299	153	598	83	179	5	45	14
Brumley, M., Det.†	.198	92	212	33	42	1	11	8
Buckner, B., K.C.*	.216	79	176	7	38	1	16	1
Buechele, S., Tex.	.235	155	486	60	114	16	59	1
Buhner, J., Sea.	.275	58	204	27	56	9	33	1
Burks, E., Bos.	.303	97	399	73	121	12	61	21
Bush, R., Min.*	.263	141	391	60	103	14	54	5
Calderon, I., Chi.	.286	157	622	83	178	14	87	7
Canale, G., Mil.*	.192	13	26	5	5	1	3	0
Canseco, J., Oak.	.269	65	227	40	61	17	57	6
Carter, J., Cle.	.243	162	651	84	158	35	105	13
Castillo, C., Min.	.257	94	218	23	56	8	33	1
Cerone, R., Bos.	.243	102	296	28	72	4	48	0
Clark, D., Cle.*	.237	102	253	21	60	8	29	0
Cochrane, D., Sea.†	.235	54	102	13	24	3	7	0
Coles, D., Sea.	.252	146	535	54	135	10	59	5
Coolbaugh, S., Tex.	.275	25	51	7	14	2	7	0
Cotto, H., Sea.	.264	100	295	44	78	9	33	10
Daugherty, J., Tex.†	.302	52	106	15	32	1	10	2
Davis, A., Sea.*	.305	142	498	84	152	21	95	0
Davis, C., Cal.†	.271	154	560	81	152	22	90	3
De los Santos, L., K.C.	.253	28	87	6	22	0	6	0
Deer, R., Mil.	.210	130	466	72	98	26	65	4
Devereaux, M., Bal.	.266	122	391	55	104	8	46	22
Diaz, M., Sea.	.135	52	74	9	10	1	7	0
Downing, B., Cal.	.283	142	544	59	154	14	59	0
Ducey, R., Tor.*	.211	41	76	5	16	0	7	2
Dwyer, J., Min.*	.316	88	225	34	71	3	23	2
Eisenreich, J., K.C.*	.293	134	475	64	139	9	59	27
Engle, D., Mil.	.215	27	65	5	14	2	8	0
Esasky, N., Bos.	.277	154	564	79	156	30	108	1
Espinoza, A., N.Y.	.282	146	503	51	142	0	41	3
Espy, C., Tex.†	.257	142	475	65	122	3	31	45

Batter and Club	AVG	G	AB	R	H	HR	RBI	SB
Evans, D., Bos.	.285	146	520	82	148	20	100	3
Felder, M., Mil.†	.241	117	315	50	76	3	23	26
Felix, J., Tor.†	.258	110	415	62	107	9	46	18
Fermin, F., Cle.	.238	156	484	50	115	0	21	6
Fernandez, T., Tor.†	.257	140	573	64	147	11	64	22
Finley, S., Bal.*	.249	81	217	35	54	2	25	17
Fisk, C., Chi.	.293	103	375	47	110	13	68	1
Fletcher, S., Tex.-Chi.	.253	142	546	77	138	1	43	2
Franco, J., Tex.	.316	150	548	80	173	13	92	21
Francona, T., Mil.*	.232	90	233	26	54	3	23	2
Gaetti, G., Min.	.251	130	498	63	125	19	75	6
Gagne, G., Min.	.272	149	460	69	125	9	48	11
Gallagher, D., Chi.	.266	161	601	74	160	1	46	5
Gallego, M., Oak.	.252	133	357	45	90	3	30	7
Gantner, J., Mil.*	.274	116	409	51	112	0	34	20
Gedman, R., Bos.*	.212	93	260	24	55	4	16	0
Geren, R., N.Y.	.288	65	205	26	59	9	27	0
Gladden, D., Min.	.295	121	461	69	136	8	46	23
Gonzales, R., Bal.	.217	71	166	16	36	1	11	5
Gonzalez, J., Tex.	.150	24	60	6	9	1	7	0
Greenwell, M., Bos.*	.308	145	578	87	178	14	95	13
Griffey, K., Sea.*	.264	127	455	61	120	16	61	16
Gruber, K., Tor.	.290	135	545	83	158	18	73	10
Guillen, O., Chi.*	.253	155	597	63	151	1	54	36
Hale, C., Min.*	.209	28	67	6	14	0	4	0
Hall, M., N.Y.*	.260	113	361	54	94	17	58	0
Harper, B., Min.	.325	126	385	43	125	8	57	2
Hassey, R., Oak.*	.228	97	268	29	61	5	23	1
Heath, M., Det.	.263	122	396	38	104	10	43	7
Heep, D., Bos.*	.300	113	320	36	96	5	49	0
Henderson, D., Oak.	.250	152	579	77	145	15	80	8
Henderson, R., N.Y.-Oak.	.274	150	541	113	148	12	57	77
Hill, G., Tor.	.288	19	52	4	15	1	7	2
Hoffman, G., Cal.	.212	48	104	9	22	1	3	0
Horn, S., Bos.*	.148	33	54	1	8	0	4	0
Howell, J., Cal.*	.228	144	474	56	108	20	52	0
Hrbek, K., Min.*	.272	109	375	59	102	25	84	3

Batter and Club	AVG	G	AB	R	H	HR	RBI	SB
Hubbard, G., Oak.	.198	53	131	12	26	3	12	2
Hulett, T., Bal.	.278	33	97	12	27	3	18	0
Incaviglia, P., Tex.	.236	133	453	48	107	21	81	5
Jackson, B., K.C.	.256	135	515	86	132	32	105	26
Jacoby, B., Cle.	.272	147	519	49	141	13	64	2
James, D., Cle.*	.306	71	245	26	75	4	29	1
Javier, S., Oak.†	.248	112	310	42	77	1	28	12
Jefferson, S., N.Y.-Bal.†	.245	45	139	20	34	4	21	10
Johnson, L., Chi.*	.300	50	180	28	54	0	16	16
Jones, T., Det.	.259	46	158	17	41	3	26	1
Jose, F., Oak.†	.193	20	57	3	11	0	5	0
Joyner, W., Cal.*	.282	159	593	78	167	16	79	3
Karkovice, R., Chi.	.264	71	182	21	48	3	24	0
Kelly, R., N.Y.	.302	137	441	65	133	9	48	35
Kingery, M., Sea.*	.224	31	76	14	17	2	6	1
Kittle, R., Chi.	.302	51	169	26	51	11	37	0
Komminsk, B., Cle.	.237	71	198	27	47	8	33	8
Kreuter, C., Tex.†	.152	87	158	16	24	5	9	0
Kunkel J., Tex.	.270	108	293	39	79	8	29	3
Kutcher, R., Bos.	.225	77	160	28	36	2	18	3
Lansford, C., Oak.	.336	148	551	81	185	2	52	37
Larkin, G., Min.†	.267	136	446	61	119	6	46	5
Laudner, T., Min.	.222	100	239	24	53	6	27	1
Lawless, T., Tor.	.229	59	70	20	16	0	3	12
Leach, R., Tex.*	.272	110	239	32	65	1	23	2
Lee, M., Tor.†	.260	99	300	27	78	3	34	4
Lemon, C., Det.	.237	127	414	45	98	7	47	1
Leonard, J., Sea.	.254	150	566	69	144	24	93	6
Liriano, N., Tor.†	.263	132	418	51	110	5	53	16
Lovullo, T., Det.†	.115	29	87	8	10	1	4	0
Lusader, S., Det.*	.252	40	103	15	26	1	8	3
Lynn, F., Det.*	.241	117	353	44	85	11	46	1
Lyons, S., Chi.*	.264	140	443	51	117	2	50	9
Macfarlane, M., K.C.	.223	69	157	13	35	2	19	0
Manrique, F., Chi.-Tex.	.294	119	378	46	111	4	52	4
Martinez, C., Chi.	.300	109	350	44	105	5	32	4
Martinez, E., Sea.	.240	65	171	20	41	2	20	2

Batter and Club	AVG	G	AB	R	H	HR	RBI	SB
Mattingly, D., N.Y.*	.303	158	631	79	191	23	113	3
Mazzilli, L., Tor.†	.227	28	66	12	15	4	11	2
McDowell, O., Cle.*	.222	69	239	33	53	3	22	12
McGriff, F., Tor.*	.269	161	551	98	148	36	92	7
McGuire, B., Sea.	.179	14	28	2	5	1	4	0
McGwire, M., Oak.	.231	143	490	74	113	33	95	1
McLemore, M., Cal.†	.243	32	103	12	25	0	14	6
Medina, L., Cle.	.205	30	83	8	17	4	8	0
Melvin, B., Bal.	.241	85	278	22	67	1	32	1
Mercado, O., Min.	.105	19	38	1	4	0	1	1
Merullo, M., Chi.*	.222	31	81	5	18	1	8	0
Meulens, H., N.Y.	.179	8	28	2	5	0	1	0
Meyer, J., Mil.	.224	53	147	13	33	7	29	1
Milligan, R., Bal.	.268	124	365	56	98	12	45	9
Molitor, P., Mil.	.315	155	615	84	194	11	56	27
Moreland, K., Det.-Bal.	.278	123	425	45	118	6	45	3
Morman, R., Chi.	.224	37	58	5	13	0	8	1
Moseby, L., Tor.*	.221	135	502	72	111	11	43	24
Moses, J., Min.†	.281	129	242	33	68	1	31	14
Mulliniks, R., Tor.*	.238	103	273	25	65	3	29	0
Myers, G., Tor.*	.114	17	44	0	5	0	1	0
Newman, A., Min.†	.253	141	446	62	113	0	38	25
Nokes, M., Det.*	.250	87	268	15	67	9	39	1
O'Brien, C., Mil.	.234	62	188	22	44	6	35	0
O'Brien, P., Cle.*	.260	155	554	75	144	12	55	3
Orsulak, J., Bal.*	.285	123	390	59	111	7	55	5
Orton, J., Cal.	.179	16	39	4	7	0	4	0
Pagliarulo, M., N.Y.*	.197	74	223	19	44	4	16	1
Palacios, R., K.C.	.170	55	47	12	8	1	8	0
Palmeiro, R., Tex.*	.275	156	559	76	154	8	64	4
Parker, D., Oak.*	.264	144	553	56	146	22	97	0
Parrish, L., Cal.	.238	124	433	48	103	17	50	1
Pasqua, D., Chi.*	.248	73	246	26	61	11	47	1
Pecota, B., K.C.	.205	65	83	21	17	3	5	5
Pedrique, A., Det.	.203	31	69	1	14	0	5	0
Petralli, G., Tex.*	.304	70	184	18	56	4	23	0
Pettis, G., Det.†	.257	119	444	77	114	1	18	43

Batter and Club	AVG	G	AB	R	H	HR	RBI	SB
Phelps, K., N.Y.-Oak.*	.242	97	194	26	47	7	29	0
Philips, T., Oak.†	.262	143	451	48	118	4	47	3
Polidor, G., Mil.	.194	79	175	15	34	0	14	3
Polonia, L., Oak.-N.Y.*	.300	125	433	70	130	3	46	22
Presley, J., Sea.	.236	117	390	42	92	12	41	0
Puckett, K., Min.	.339	159	635	75	215	9	85	11
Quintana, C., Bos.	.208	34	77	6	16	0	6	0
Quirk, J., N.Y.-Bal.*	.176	47	85	6	15	1	10	0
Ray, J., Cal.†	.289	134	530	52	153	5	62	6
Reed, J., Bos.	.288	146	524	76	151	3	40	4
Reynolds, H., Sea.†	.300	153	613	87	184	0	43	25
Rice J., Bos.	.234	56	209	22	49	3	28	1
Richie, R., Det.*	.265	19	49	6	13	1	10	0
Ripken, B., Bal.	.239	115	318	31	76	2	26	1
Ripken, C., Bal.	.257	162	646	80	166	21	93	3
Rivera, L., Bos.	.257	93	323	35	83	5	29	2
Robidoux, B., Chi.*	.128	16	39	2	5	0	1	0
Romero, E., Bos.-Mil.	.209	61	163	17	34	0	9	0
Romine, K., Bos.	.274	92	274	30	75	1	23	1
Rose, B., Cal.	.211	14	38	4	8	1	3	0
Salas, M., Cle.*	.221	30	77	4	17	2	7	0
Sanders, D., N.Y.*	.234	14	47	7	11	2	7	1
Sax, S., N.Y.	.315	158	651	88	205	5	63	43
Schofield, D., Cal.	.228	91	302	42	69	4	26	9
Schroeder, B., Cal.	.203	41	138	16	28	6	15	0
Schu, R., Bal.-Det.	.214	99	266	25	57	7	21	1
Seitzer, K., K.C.	.281	160	597	78	168	4	48	17
Sheets, L., Bal.*	.243	102	304	33	74	7	33	1
Sheffield, G., Mil.	.247	95	368	34	91	5	32	10
Sheridan, P., Det.*	.242	50	120	16	29	3	15	4
Sierra, R., Tex.†	.306	162	634	101	194	29	119	8
Skinner, J., Cle.	.230	79	178	10	41	1	13	1
Slaught, D., N.Y.	.251	117	350	34	88	5	38	1
Snyder, C., Cle.	.215	132	489	49	105	18	59	6
Sosa, S., Tex.-Chi.	.257	58	183	27	47	4	13	7
Spiers, B., Mil.*	.255	114	345	44	88	4	33	10
Stanley, M., Tex.	.246	67	122	9	30	1	11	1

Batter and Club	AVG	G	AB	R	H	HR	RBI	SB
Steinbach, T., Oak.	.273	130	454	37	124	7	42	1
Stillwell, K., K.C.†	.261	130	463	52	121	7	54	9
Stone, J., Tex.-Bos.*	.176	40	51	8	9	0	6	3
Strange, D., Det.†	.214	64	196	16	42	1	14	3
Sundberg, J., Tex.	.197	76	147	13	29	2	8	0
Surhoff, B., Mil.*	.248	126	436	42	108	5	55	14
Tabler, P., K.C.	.259	123	390	36	101	2	42	0
Tartabull, D., K.C.	.268	133	441	54	118	18	62	4
Tettleton, M., Bal.†	.258	117	411	72	106	26	65	3
Thurman, G., K.C.	.195	72	87	24	17	0	5	16
Tolleson, W., N.Y.†	.164	80	140	16	23	1	9	5
Traber, J., Bal.*	.209	86	234	14	49	4	26	4
Trammell, A., Det.	.243	121	449	54	109	5	43	10
Valle, D., Sea.	.237	94	316	32	75	7	34	0
Vaughn, G., Mil.	.265	38	113	18	30	5	23	4
Velarde, R., N.Y.	.340	33	100	12	34	2	11	0
Venable, M., Cal.*	.358	20	53	7	19	0	4	0
Ventura, R., Chi.*	.178	16	45	5	8	0	7	0
Vizquel, O., Sea.†	.220	143	387	45	85	1	20	1
Walker, G., Chi.*	.210	77	233	25	49	5	26	0
Ward, G., N.Y.-Det.	.253	113	292	27	74	9	30	1
Washington, C., Cal.*	.273	110	418	53	114	13	42	13
Weiss, W., Oak.†	.233	84	236	30	55	3	21	6
Wellman, B., K.C.	.230	103	178	30	41	2	12	5
Whitaker, L., Det.*	.251	148	509	77	128	28	85	6
White, D., Cal.†	.245	156	636	86	156	12	56	44
White, F., K.C.	.256	135	418	34	107	2	36	3
Whitt, E., Tor.*	.262	129	385	42	101	11	53	5
Williams, E., Chi.	.274	66	201	25	55	3	10	1
Williams, K., Det.	.205	94	258	29	53	6	23	9
Wilson, M., Tor.†	.298	54	238	32	71	2	17	12
Wilson, W., K.C.†	.253	112	383	58	97	3	43	24
Winters, M., K.C.*	.234	42	107	14	25	2	9	0
Worthington, C., Bal.	.247	145	497	57	123	15	70	1
Young, M., Cle.†	.186	32	59	2	11	1	5	1
Yount, R., Mil.	.318	160	614	101	195	21	103	19
Zuvella, P., Cle.	.276	24	58	10	16	2	6	0

AMERICAN LEAGUE
Pitching

(80 or more innings pitched)
*Throws left-handed

Pitcher and Club	W	L	ERA	G	IP	H	BB	SO
Abbott, J., Cal.*	12	12	3.92	29	181.1	190	74	115
Alexander, D., Det.	6	18	4.44	33	223.0	245	76	95
Anderson, A., Min.*	17	10	3.80	33	196.2	214	53	69
Aquino, L., K.C.	6	8	3.50	34	141.1	148	35	68
August, D., Mil.	12	12	5.31	31	142.1	175	58	51
Bailes, S., Cle.*	5	9	4.28	34	113.2	116	29	47
Ballard, J., Bal.*	18	8	3.43	35	215.1	240	57	62
Bankhead, S., Sea.	14	6	3.34	33	210.1	187	63	140
Berenguer, J., Min.	9	3	3.48	56	106.0	96	47	93
Black, B., Cle.*	12	11	3.36	33	222.1	213	52	88
Blyleven, B., Cal.	17	5	2.73	33	241.0	225	44	131
Boddicker, M., Bos.	15	11	4.00	34	211.2	217	71	145
Bosio, C., Mil.	15	10	2.95	33	234.2	225	48	173
Brown, K., Tex.	12	9	3.35	28	191.0	167	70	104
Burns, T., Oak.	6	5	2.24	50	96.1	66	28	49
Cadaret, G., Oak.-N.Y.* ..	5	5	4.05	46	120.0	130	57	80
Candiotti, T., Cle.	13	10	3.10	31	206.0	188	55	124
Cary, C., N.Y.*	4	4	3.26	22	99.1	78	29	79
Cerutti, J., Tor.*	11	11	3.07	33	205.1	214	53	69
Clemens, R., Bos.	17	11	3.13	35	253.1	215	93	230
Crim, C., Mil.	9	7	2.83	76	117.2	114	36	59
Davis, S., Oak.	19	7	4.36	31	169.1	187	68	91
Dopson, J., Bos.	12	8	3.99	29	169.1	166	69	95
Dotson, R., N.Y.-Chi.	5	12	4.46	28	151.1	181	58	69
Dunne, M., Sea.	2	9	5.27	15	85.1	104	37	38
Farrell, J., Cle.	9	14	3.63	31	208.0	196	71	132
Finley, C., Cal.*	16	9	2.57	29	199.2	171	82	156
Flanagan, M., Tor.*	8	10	3.93	30	171.2	186	47	47
Fraser, W., Cal.	4	7	3.24	44	91.2	80	23	46
Gardner, W., Bos.	3	7	5.97	22	86.0	97	47	81
Gibson, P., Det.*	4	8	4.64	45	132.0	129	57	77

Pitcher and Club	W	L	ERA	G	IP	H	BB	SO
Gordon, T., K.C.	17	9	3.64	49	163.0	122	86	153
Gubicza, M., K.C.	15	11	3.04	36	255.0	252	63	173
Guetterman, L., N.Y.*	5	5	2.45	70	103.0	98	26	51
Hanson, E., Sea.	9	5	3.18	17	113.1	103	32	75
Harnisch, P., Bal.	5	9	4.62	18	103.1	97	64	70
Hawkins, A., N.Y.	15	15	4.80	34	208.1	238	76	98
Henke, T., Tor.	8	3	1.92	64	89.0	66	25	116
Henneman, M., Det.	11	4	3.70	60	90.0	84	51	69
Hibbard, G., Chi.*	6	7	3.21	23	137.1	142	41	55
Higuera, T., Mil.*	9	6	3.46	22	135.1	125	48	91
Hillegas, S., Chi.	7	11	4.74	50	119.2	132	51	76
Holman, B., Sea.	8	10	3.44	23	159.2	160	62	82
Holton, B., Bal.	5	7	4.02	39	116.1	140	39	51
Hough, C., Tex.	10	13	4.35	30	182.0	168	95	94
Jackson, M., Sea.	4	6	3.17	65	99.1	81	54	94
Jeffcoat, M., Tex.*	9	6	3.58	22	130.2	139	33	64
Johnson, D., Bal.	4	7	4.23	14	89.1	90	28	26
Johnson, R., Sea.*	7	9	4.40	22	131.0	118	70	104
Jones, D., Cle.	7	10	2.34	59	80.2	76	13	65
Key, J. Tor.*	13	14	3.88	33	216.0	226	27	118
King, E., Chi.	9	10	3.39	25	159.1	144	64	72
Knudson, M., Mil.	8	5	3.35	40	123.2	110	29	47
Krueger, B., Mil.*	3	2	3.84	34	93.2	96	33	72
LaPoint, D., N.Y.*	6	9	5.62	20	113.2	146	45	51
Lamp, D., Bos.	4	2	2.32	42	112.1	96	27	61
Leibrandt, C., K.C.*	5	11	5.14	33	161.0	196	54	73
Long, B., Chi.	5	5	3.92	30	98.2	101	37	51
McCaskill, K., Cal.	15	10	2.93	32	212.0	202	59	107
McCullers, L., N.Y.	4	3	4.57	52	84.2	83	37	82
Milacki, B., Bal.	14	12	3.74	37	243.0	233	88	113
Minton, G., Cal.	4	3	2.20	62	90.0	76	37	42
Montgomery, J., K.C.	7	3	1.37	63	92.0	66	25	94
Moore, M., Oak.	19	11	2.61	35	241.2	193	83	172
Morris, J., Det.	6	14	4.86	24	170.1	189	59	115
Murphy, R., Bos.*	5	7	2.74	74	105.0	97	41	107
Navarro, J., Mil.	7	8	3.12	19	109.2	119	32	56
Nelson, G., Oak.	3	5	3.26	50	80.0	60	30	70

Pitcher and Club	W	L	ERA	G	IP	H	BB	SO
Olson, G., Bal.	5	2	1.69	64	85.0	57	46	90
Pall, D., Chi.	4	5	3.31	53	87.0	90	19	58
Parker, C., N.Y.	4	5	3.68	22	120.0	123	31	53
Perez, M., Chi.	11	14	5.01	31	183.1	187	90	141
Plunk, E., Oak.-N.Y.	8	6	3.28	50	104.1	82	64	85
Rawley, S., Min.*	5	12	5.21	27	145.0	167	60	68
Reed, J., Sea.	7	7	3.19	52	101.2	89	43	50
Reuss, J., Chi.-Mil.*	9	9	5.13	30	140.1	171	34	40
Rosenberg, S., Chi.*	4	13	4.94	38	142.0	148	58	77
Ryan, N., Tex.	16	10	3.20	32	239.1	162	98	301
Saberhagen, B., K.C.	23	6	2.16	36	262.1	209	43	193
Schmidt, D., Bal.	10	13	5.69	38	156.2	196	36	46
Smith, R., Min.	10	6	3.92	32	172.1	180	51	92
Smithson, M., Bos.	7	14	4.95	40	143.2	170	35	61
Stewart, D., Oak.	21	9	3.32	36	257.2	260	69	155
Stieb, D., Tor.	17	8	3.35	33	206.2	164	76	101
Stottlemyre, T., Tor.	7	7	3.88	27	127.2	137	44	63
Swift, B., Sea.	7	3	4.43	37	130.0	140	38	45
Swindell, G., Cle.*	13	6	3.37	28	184.1	170	51	129
Tanana, F., Det.*	10	14	3.58	33	223.2	227	74	147
Terrell, W., N.Y.	6	5	5.20	13	83.0	102	24	30
Thurmond, M., Bal.*	2	4	3.90	49	90.0	102	17	34
Viola, F., Min.*	8	12	3.79	24	175.2	171	47	138
Ward, D., Tor.	4	10	3.77	66	114.2	94	58	122
Welch, B., Oak.	17	8	3.00	33	209.2	191	78	137
Wells, D., Tor.*	7	4	2.40	54	86.1	66	28	78
Williamson, M., Bal.	10	5	2.93	65	107.1	105	30	55
Witt, B., Tex.	12	13	5.14	31	194.1	182	114	166
Witt, M., Cal.	9	15	4.54	33	220.0	252	48	123
Yett, R., Cle.	5	6	5.00	32	99.0	111	47	47
Young, C., Oak.*	5	9	3.73	25	110.0	117	47	55

NATIONAL LEAGUE
Batting

(39 or more at-bats)
*Bats Left-Handed †Switch-Hitter

Batter and Club	AVG	G	AB	R	H	HR	RBI	SB
Abner, S., S.D.	.176	57	102	13	18	2	14	1
Aldrete, M., Mon.*	.221	76	136	12	30	1	12	1
Alomar, R., S.D.†	.295	158	623	82	184	7	56	42
Anderson, D., L.A.	.229	87	140	15	32	1	14	2
Anthony, E., Hou.*	.180	25	61	7	11	4	7	0
Ashby, A., Hou.	.164	22	61	4	10	0	3	0
Bass, K., Hou.†	.300	87	313	42	94	5	44	11
Bean, B., L.A.*	.197	51	71	7	14	0	3	0
Belcher, T., L.A.	.100	39	70	3	7	0	6	0
Bell, J., Pit.	.258	78	271	33	70	2	27	5
Belliard, R., Pit.	.214	67	154	10	33	0	8	5
Benedict, B., Atl.	.194	66	160	12	31	1	6	0
Benzinger, T., Cin.†	.245	161	628	79	154	17	76	3
Berroa, G., Atl.	.265	81	136	7	36	2	9	0
Berryhill, D., Chi.	.257	91	334	37	86	5	41	1
Bielecki, M., Chi.	.043	33	70	1	3	0	3	1
Biggio, C., Hou.	.257	134	443	64	114	13	60	21
Bilardello, D., Pit.	.225	33	80	11	18	2	8	1
Blauser, J., Atl.	.270	142	456	63	123	12	46	5
Bonds, B., Pit.	.248	159	580	96	144	19	58	32
Bonilla, B., Pit.†	.281	163	616	96	173	24	86	8
Brooks, H., Mon.	.268	148	542	56	145	14	70	6
Browning, T., Cin.*	.090	41	78	2	7	0	2	0
Brunansky, T., St.L.	.239	158	556	67	133	20	85	5
Butler, B., S.F.*	.283	154	594	100	168	4	36	31
Caminiti, K., Hou.†	.255	161	585	71	149	10	72	4
Cangelosi, J., Pit.†	.219	112	160	18	35	0	9	11
Carreon, M., N.Y.	.308	68	133	20	41	6	16	2
Carter, G., N.Y.	.183	50	153	14	28	2	15	0
Clancy, J., Hou.	.146	33	41	3	6	0	0	0

Batter and Club	AVG	G	AB	R	H	HR	RBI	SB
Clark, Ja., S.D.	.242	142	455	76	110	26	94	6
Clark, Je., S.D.	.195	17	41	5	8	1	7	0
Clark, W., S.F.*	.333	159	588	104	196	23	111	8
Coleman, V., St.L.†	.254	145	563	94	143	2	28	65
Collins, D., Cin.†	.236	78	106	12	25	0	7	3
Cone, D., N.Y.*	.234	34	77	9	18	0	4	0
Cook, D., S.F.-Phi.*	.214	24	42	4	9	0	3	0
Daniels, K., Cin.-L.A.*	.246	55	171	33	42	4	17	9
Darling, R., N.Y.	.123	35	73	8	9	2	5	0
Dascenzo, D., Chi.†	.165	47	139	20	23	1	12	6
Daulton, D., Phi.*	.201	131	368	29	74	8	44	2
Davidson, M., Hou.	.200	33	65	7	13	1	5	1
Davis, E., Cin.	.281	131	462	74	130	34	101	21
Davis, G., Hou.	.269	158	581	87	156	34	89	4
Davis, J., Atl.	.169	78	231	12	39	4	19	0
Davis, M., L.A.*	.249	67	173	21	43	5	19	6
Dawson, A., Chi.	.252	118	416	62	105	21	77	8
DeLeon, J., St.L.	.096	36	83	3	8	0	1	0
Dempsey, R., L.A.	.179	79	151	16	27	4	16	1
Dernier, B., Phi.	.171	107	187	26	32	1	13	4
Deshaies, J., Hou.*	.120	35	75	2	9	0	2	0
Diaz, B., Cin.	.205	43	132	6	27	1	8	0
Distefano, B., Pit.	.247	96	154	12	38	2	15	1
Doran, B., Hou.†	.219	142	507	65	111	8	58	22
Drabek, D., Pit.	.104	40	77	1	8	0	3	0
Duncan, M., L.A.-Cin.	.248	94	258	32	64	3	21	9
Dunston, S., Chi.	.278	138	471	52	131	9	60	19
Dykstra, L., N.Y.-Phi.*	.237	146	511	66	121	7	32	30
Elster, K., N.Y.	.231	151	458	52	106	10	55	4
Evans, D., Atl.*	.207	107	276	31	57	11	39	0
Fernandez, S., N.Y.*	.211	35	71	2	15	1	8	0
Fitzgerald, M., Mon.	.238	100	290	33	69	7	42	3
Flannery, T., S.D.*	.231	73	130	9	30	0	8	2
Foley, T., Mon.*	.229	122	375	34	86	7	39	2
Ford, C., Phi.*	.218	108	142	13	31	1	13	5
Galarraga, A., Mon.	.257	152	572	76	147	23	85	12
Gant, R., Atl.	.177	75	260	26	46	9	25	9

Batter and Club	AVG	G	AB	R	H	HR	RBI	SB
Garcia, D., Mon.	.271	80	203	26	55	3	18	5
Garrelts, S., S.F.	.136	32	66	3	9	0	2	1
Gibson, K., L.A.*	.213	71	253	35	54	9	28	12
Girardi, J., Chi.	.248	59	157	15	39	1	14	2
Glavine, T., Atl.*	.149	30	67	6	10	0	4	0
Gonzalez, J., L.A.	.268	95	261	31	70	3	18	9
Gooden, D., N.Y.	.200	19	40	1	8	0	1	0
Grace, M., Chi.*	.314	142	510	74	160	13	79	14
Gregg, T., Atl.*	.243	102	276	24	67	6	23	3
Griffey, K., Cin.*	.263	106	236	26	62	8	30	4
Griffin, A., L.A.†	.247	136	506	49	125	0	29	10
Grissom, M., Mon.	.257	26	74	16	19	1	2	1
Gross, G., Hou.*	.200	60	75	2	15	0	4	0
Gross, K, Mon.	.141	31	64	5	9	0	1	0
Guerrero, P., St.L.	.311	162	570	60	177	17	117	2
Gwynn, C., L.A.*	.235	32	68	8	16	0	7	1
Gwynn, T., S.D.*	.336	158	604	82	203	4	62	40
Hamilton, J., L.A.	.245	151	548	45	134	12	56	0
Harris, L., Cin.-L.A.*	.236	115	335	36	79	3	26	14
Hatcher, B., Hou.-Pit.	.231	135	481	59	111	4	51	24
Hatcher, M., L.A.	.295	94	224	18	66	2	25	1
Hayes, C., S.F.-Phi.	.257	87	304	26	78	8	43	3
Hayes, V., Phi.*	.259	154	540	93	140	26	78	28
Heaton, N., Pit.*	.214	44	42	2	9	0	2	0
Hernandez, K., N.Y.*	.233	75	215	18	50	4	19	0
Herr, T., Phi.†	.287	151	561	65	161	2	37	10
Hershiser, O., L.A.	.182	35	77	4	14	0	2	0
Hill, K., St.L.	.153	33	59	4	9	0	3	0
Howell, K., Phi.	.092	33	65	0	6	0	1	0
Hudler, R., Mon.	.245	92	155	21	38	6	13	15
Hurst, B., S.D.*	.071	33	70	4	5	0	0	0
Huson, J., Mon.*	.162	32	74	1	12	0	2	3
Jackson, D., Chi-S.D.	.218	70	170	17	37	4	20	1
James C., Phi.-S.D.	.243	132	482	55	117	13	65	5
James, D., Atl.*	.259	63	170	15	44	1	11	1
Jefferies, G., N.Y.†	.258	141	508	72	131	12	56	21
Jeltz, S., Phi.†	.243	116	263	28	64	4	25	4

Batter and Club	AVG	G	AB	R	H	HR	RBI	SB
Johnson, H., N.Y.†	.287	153	571	104	164	36	101	41
Johnson, W., Mon.†	.272	85	114	9	31	2	17	1
Jones, T., S.F.	.186	40	97	5	18	0	12	2
Jones, T., St.L.*	.293	42	75	11	22	0	7	1
Jordan, R., Phi.	.285	144	523	63	149	12	75	4
Jurak, E., S.F.	.238	30	42	2	10	0	1	0
Justice, D., Atl.*	.235	16	51	7	12	1	3	2
Kennedy, T., S.F.	.239	125	355	19	85	5	34	1
Kilgus, P., Chi.*	.073	35	41	1	3	0	2	0
King, J., Pit.	.195	75	215	31	42	5	19	4
Knepper, B., Hou.-S.F.	.186	35	43	5	8	1	3	0
Kruk, J., S.D.-Phi.*	.300	112	357	53	107	8	44	3
LaCoss, M., S.F.	.073	45	41	1	3	0	1	0
Lake, S., Phi.	.252	58	155	9	39	2	14	0
Langston, M., Mon.	.172	24	64	4	11	0	3	0
Larkin, B., Cin.	.342	97	325	47	111	4	36	10
LaValliere, M., Pit.*	.316	68	190	15	60	2	23	0
Law, V., Chi.	.235	130	408	38	96	7	42	2
Leary, T., L.A.-Cin.	.119	33	59	2	7	0	4	0
Lemke, M., Atl.†	.182	14	55	4	10	2	10	0
Lilliquist, D., Atl.*	.190	36	63	5	12	0	4	0
Lind, J., Pit.	.232	153	578	52	134	2	48	15
Lindeman, J., St.L.	.111	73	45	8	5	0	2	0
Litton, G., S.F.	.252	71	143	12	36	4	17	0
Lombardi, P., N.Y.	.229	18	48	4	11	1	3	0
Lyons, B., N.Y.	.247	79	235	15	58	3	27	0
Maddux, G., Chi.	.210	35	81	6	17	0	4	1
Madison, S., Cin.†	.173	40	98	13	17	1	7	0
Magadan, D., N.Y.*	.286	127	374	47	107	4	41	1
Magrane, J., St.L.	.138	38	80	6	11	1	4	0
Mahler, R., Cin.	.177	40	62	4	11	0	1	0
Maldonado, C., S.F.	.217	129	345	39	75	9	41	4
Manwaring, K., S.F.	.210	85	200	14	42	0	18	2
Marshall, M., L.A.	.260	105	377	41	98	11	42	2
Martinez, C., S.D.	.221	111	267	23	59	6	39	0
Martinez, Da., Mon.*	.274	126	361	41	99	3	27	23
Martinez, De., Mon.	.125	34	72	5	9	0	3	1

Batter and Club	AVG	G	AB	R	H	HR	RBI	SB
Mazzilli, L., N.Y.†	.183	48	60	10	11	2	7	3
McClendon, L., Chi.	.286	92	259	47	74	12	40	6
McDowell, O., Atl.*	.304	76	280	56	85	7	24	15
McGee, W., St.L.†	.236	58	199	23	47	3	17	8
McReynolds, K., N.Y.	.272	148	545	74	148	22	85	15
Meadows, L., Hou.*	.176	31	51	5	9	3	10	1
Miller, K., N.Y.	.231	57	143	15	33	1	7	6
Mitchell, K., S.F.	.291	154	543	100	158	47	125	3
Morris., J., St.L.*	.239	96	117	8	28	2	14	1
Murphy, D., Phi.*	.218	98	156	20	34	9	27	0
Murphy, D., Atl.	.228	154	574	60	131	20	84	3
Murray, E., L.A.†	.247	160	594	66	147	20	88	7
Nelson, R., S.D.*	.195	42	82	6	16	3	7	1
Nixon, D., S.F.	.265	95	166	23	44	1	15	10
Nixon, O., Mon.†	.217	126	258	41	56	0	21	37
Noboa, J., Mon.	.227	21	44	3	10	0	1	0
O'Neill, P., Cin.*	.276	117	428	49	118	15	74	20
Oberkfell, K., Pit.-S.F.*	.269	97	156	19	42	2	17	0
Oester, R., Cin.†	.246	109	305	23	75	1	14	1
Ojeda, B., N.Y.*	.106	32	66	3	7	0	0	0
Oliver, J., Cin.	.272	49	151	13	41	3	23	0
Oquendo, J., St.L.†	.291	163	556	59	162	1	48	3
Ortiz, J., Pit.	.217	91	230	16	50	1	22	2
Owen, S., Mon.†	.233	142	437	52	102	6	41	3
Pagliarulo, M., S.D.*	.196	50	148	12	29	3	14	2
Pagnozzi, T., St.L.	.150	52	80	3	12	0	3	0
Parent, M., S.D.	.191	52	141	12	27	7	21	1
Pena, T., St.L.	.259	141	424	36	110	4	37	5
Pendleton, T., St.L.†	.264	162	613	83	162	13	74	9
Perez, P., Mon.	.204	35	54	2	11	0	8	0
Perry, G., Atl.*	.252	72	266	24	67	4	21	10
Pevey, M., Mon.*	.220	13	41	2	9	0	3	0
Prince, T., Pit.	.135	21	52	1	7	0	5	1
Puhl, T., Hou.*	.271	121	354	41	96	0	27	9
Quinones, L., Cin.†	.244	97	340	43	83	12	34	2
Quinones, R., Pit.	.209	71	225	21	47	3	29	0
Raines, T., Mon.†	.286	145	517	76	148	9	60	41

Batter and Club	AVG	G	AB	R	H	HR	RBI	SB
Ramirez, R., Hou.	.246	151	537	46	132	6	54	3
Ramos, D., Chi.	.263	85	179	18	47	1	19	1
Randolph, W., L.A.	.282	145	549	62	155	2	36	7
Rasmussen, D., S.D.*	.169	33	65	1	11	0	2	0
Ready, R., S.D.-Phi.	.264	100	254	37	67	8	26	4
Redus, G., Pit.	.283	98	279	42	79	6	33	25
Reed J., Cin.*	.223	102	287	16	64	3	23	0
Reuschel, R., S.F.	.164	32	61	2	10	0	3	0
Reynolds, C., Hou.	.201	101	189	16	38	2	14	1
Reynolds, R., Pit.†	.270	125	363	45	98	6	48	22
Richardson, J., Cin.	.168	53	125	10	21	2	11	1
Rijo, J., Cin.	.211	19	38	0	8	0	1	1
Riles, E., S.F.*	.278	122	302	43	84	7	40	0
Roberts, L., S.D.†	.301	117	329	81	99	3	25	21
Robinson, D., S.F.	.185	40	81	7	15	3	7	0
Roomes, R., Cin.	.263	107	315	36	83	7	34	12
Russell, J., Atl.	.182	74	159	14	29	2	9	0
Sabo, C., Cin.	.260	82	304	40	79	6	29	14
Salazar, L., S.D.-Chi.	.282	121	326	34	92	9	34	1
Samuel, J., Phi.-N.Y.	.235	137	532	69	125	11	48	42
Sandberg, R., Chi.	.290	157	606	104	176	30	76	15
Sanderson, S., Chi.	.047	37	43	1	2	0	1	0
Santiago, B., S.D.	.236	129	462	50	109	16	62	11
Santovenia, N., Mon.	.250	97	304	30	76	5	31	2
Sasser, M., N.Y.*	.291	72	182	17	53	1	22	0
Schmidt, M., Phi.	.203	42	148	19	30	6	28	0
Scioscia, M., L.A.*	.250	133	408	40	102	10	44	0
Scott, M., Hou.	.133	33	75	2	10	1	10	0
Shelby, J., L.A.†	.183	108	345	28	63	1	12	10
Sheridan, P., S.F.*	.205	70	161	20	33	3	14	4
Smiley, J., Pit.*	.138	28	65	0	9	0	7	0
Smith, B., Mon.	.065	33	62	4	4	0	4	0
Smith, D., Chi.*	.324	109	343	52	111	9	52	9
Smith, L., Atl.	.315	134	482	89	152	21	79	25
Smith, O., St.L.†	.273	155	593	82	162	2	50	29
Smith, P., Atl.	.098	29	41	2	4	0	3	0
Smoltz, J., Atl.	.113	33	62	6	7	1	6	0

Batter and Club	AVG	G	AB	R	H	HR	RBI	SB
Strawberry D., N.Y.*	.225	134	476	69	107	29	77	11
Stubbs, F., L.A.*	.291	69	103	11	30	4	15	3
Sutcliffe, R., Chi.*	.143	37	70	5	10	0	5	2
Templeton, G., S.D.†	.255	142	506	43	129	6	40	1
Terrell, W., S.D.*	.100	19	40	2	4	0	2	0
Terry, S., St.L.	.156	35	45	3	7	2	4	0
Teufel, T., N.Y.	.256	83	219	27	56	2	15	1
Thomas A., Atl.	.213	141	554	41	118	13	57	3
Thompson, M., St.L.*	.290	155	545	60	158	4	68	27
Thompson, R., S.F.	.241	148	547	91	132	13	50	12
Thon, D., Phi.	.271	136	435	45	118	15	60	6
Treadway, J., Atl.*	.277	134	473	58	131	8	40	3
Trevino, A., Hou.	.290	59	131	15	38	2	16	0
Trillo, M., Cin.	.205	17	39	3	8	0	0	0
Uribe, J., S.F.†	.221	151	453	34	100	1	30	6
Valenzuela, F., L.A.*	.182	34	66	3	12	0	6	0
Van Slyke, A., Pit.*	.237	130	476	64	113	9	53	16
Varsho, G., Chi.*	.184	61	87	10	16	0	6	3
Walker, L., Mon.*	.170	20	47	4	8	0	4	1
Wallach, T., Mon.	.277	154	573	76	159	13	77	3
Walling, D., St.L.*	.304	69	79	9	24	1	11	0
Walton, J., Chi.	.293	116	475	64	139	5	46	24
Webster, M., Chi.†	.257	98	272	40	70	3	19	14
Wetherby, J., Atl.*	.208	52	48	5	10	1	7	1
Whited, E., Atl.	.162	36	74	5	12	1	4	1
Whitson, E., S.D.	.139	36	72	4	10	0	4	0
Wilkerson, C., Chi.†	.244	77	160	18	39	1	10	4
Williams, M., S.F.	.202	84	292	31	59	18	50	1
Wilson, G., Pit.-Hou.	.266	128	432	50	115	11	64	1
Wilson, M., N.Y.†	.205	80	249	22	51	3	18	7
Winningham, H., Cin.*	.251	115	251	40	63	3	13	14
Wrona, R., Chi.	.283	38	92	11	26	2	14	0
Wynne, M., S.D.-Chi.*	.243	125	342	27	83	7	39	6
Yelding, E., Hou.	.233	70	90	19	21	0	9	11
Young, G., Hou.†	.233	146	533	71	124	0	38	34
Youngblood, J., Cin.	.212	76	118	13	25	3	13	0
Zeile, T., St.L.	.256	28	82	7	21	1	8	0

NATIONAL LEAGUE
Pitching

(30 or more innings pitched)
*Throws Left-handed

Pitcher and Club	W	L	ERA	G	IP	H	BB	SO
Aase, D., N.Y.	1	5	3.94	49	59.1	56	26	34
Acker, J., Atl.	0	6	2.67	59	97.2	84	20	68
Agosto, J., Hou.*	4	5	2.93	71	83.0	81	32	46
Aguilera, R., N.Y.	6	6	2.34	36	69.1	59	21	80
Alvarez, J., Atl.	3	3	2.86	30	50.1	44	24	45
Andersen, L., Hou.	4	4	1.54	60	87.2	63	24	85
Armstrong, J., Cin.	2	3	4.64	9	42.2	40	21	23
Assenmacher, P., Atl.-Chi.*	3	4	3.99	63	76.2	74	28	79
Bair, D., Pit.	2	3	2.27	44	67.1	52	28	56
Bedrosian, S., Phi.-S.F. ...	3	7	2.87	68	84.2	56	39	58
Belcher, T., L.A. 15		12	2.82	39	230.0	182	80	200
Benes, A., S.D.	6	3	3.51	10	66.2	51	31	66
Bielecki, M., Chi. 18		7	3.14	33	212.1	187	81	147
Birtsas, T., Cin.*	2	2	3.75	42	69.2	68	27	57
Boever, J., Atl.	4	11	3.94	66	82.1	78	34	68
Brantley, J., S.F.	7	1	4.07	59	97.1	101	37	69
Browning, T., Cin.* ...15		12	3.39	37	249.2	241	64	118
Burke, T., Mon.	9	3	2.55	68	84.2	68	22	54
Carman, D., Phi.*	5	15	5.24	49	149.1	152	86	81
Carpenter, C., St.L.	4	4	3.18	36	68.0	70	26	35
Charlton, N., Cin.*	8	3	2.93	69	95.1	67	40	98
Clancy, J., Hou.	7	14	5.08	33	147.0	155	66	91
Clary, M., Atl.	4	3	3.15	18	108.2	103	31	30
Clements, P., S.D.*	4	1	3.92	23	39.0	39	15	18
Combs, P., Phi.*	4	0	2.09	6	38.2	36	6	30
Cone, D., N.Y. 14		8	3.52	34	219.2	183	74	190
Cook, D., S.F.-Phi.*	7	8	3.72	23	121.1	110	38	67
Costello, J., St.L.	5	4	3.32	48	62.1	48	20	40
Crews, T., L.A.	0	1	3.21	44	61.2	69	23	56
Darling, R., N.Y. 14		14	3.52	33	217.1	214	70	153

Pitcher and Club	W	L	ERA	G	IP	H	BB	SO
Darwin, D., Hou. 11		4	2.36	68	122.0	92	33	104
Davis, M., S.D.* 4		3	1.85	70	92.2	66	31	92
Dayley, K., St.L.* 4		3	2.87	71	75.1	63	30	40
DeLeon, J., St.L. 16		12	3.05	36	244.2	173	80	201
Deshaies, J., Hou.* 15		10	2.91	34	225.2	180	79	153
Dibble, R., Cin. 10		5	2.09	74	99.0	62	39	141
DiPino, F., St.L.* 9		0	2.45	67	88.1	73	20	44
Downs, K., S.F. 4		8	4.79	18	82.2	82	26	49
Drabek, D., Pit. 14		12	2.80	35	244.1	215	69	123
Eichhorn, M., Atl. 5		5	4.35	45	68.1	70	19	49
Fernandez, S., N.Y.* 14		5	2.83	35	219.1	157	75	198
Forsch, B., Hou. 4		5	5.32	37	108.1	133	46	40
Franco, J., Cin.* 4		8	3.12	60	80.2	77	36	60
Frohwirth, T., Phi. 1		0	3.59	45	62.2	56	18	39
Garrelts, S., S.F. 14		5	2.28	30	193.1	149	46	119
Glavine, T., Atl.* 14		8	3.68	29	186.0	172	40	90
Gooden, D., N.Y. 9		4	2.89	19	118.1	93	47	101
Gossage, R., S.F. 2		1	2.68	31	43.2	32	27	24
Grant, M., S.D. 8		2	3.33	50	116.1	105	32	69
Gross, K., Mon. 11		12	4.38	31	201.1	188	88	158
Hammaker, A., S.F.* 6		6	3.76	28	76.2	78	23	30
Harris, G., Phi. 2		2	3.58	44	75.1	64	43	51
Harris, G., S.D. 8		9	2.60	56	135.0	106	52	106
Heaton, N., Pit.* 6		7	3.05	42	147.1	127	55	67
Henry, D., Atl. 0		2	4.26	12	12.2	12	5	16
Hershiser, O., L.A. 15		15	2.31	35	256.2	226	77	178
Hesketh, J., Mon.* 6		4	5.77	43	48.1	54	26	44
Hill, K., St.L. 7		15	3.80	33	196.2	186	99	112
Holman, B., Mon. 1		2	4.83	10	31.2	34	15	23
Horton, R., L.A.-St.L.* ... 0		3	4.85	34	72.1	85	21	26
Howell, J., L.A. 5		3	1.58	56	79.2	60	22	55
Howell, K., Phi. 12		12	3.44	33	204.0	155	86	164
Hurst, B., S.D.* 15		11	2.69	33	244.2	214	66	179
Innis, J., N.Y. 0		1	3.18	29	39.2	38	8	16
Jackson, D., Cin.* 6		11	5.60	20	115.2	122	57	70
Kilgus, P., Chi.* 6		10	4.39	35	145.2	164	49	61
Kipper, B., Pit.* 3		4	2.93	52	83.0	55	33	58

Pitcher and Club	W	L	ERA	G	IP	H	BB	SO
Knepper, B., Hou.-S.F.* ..	7	12	5.13	35	165.0	190	75	64
Kramer, R., Pit.	5	9	3.96	35	111.1	90	61	52
Krukow, M., S.F.	4	3	3.98	8	43.0	37	18	18
LaCoss, M., S.F. 10		10	3.17	45	150.1	143	65	78
Lancaster, L., Chi.	4	2	1.36	42	72.2	60	15	56
Landrum, B., Pit.	2	3	1.67	56	81.0	60	28	51
Langston, M., Mon.*	12	9	2.39	24	176.2	138	93	175
Leary, T., L.A.-Cin.	8	14	3.52	33	207.0	205	68	123
Lefferts, C., S.F.*	2	4	2.69	70	107.0	93	22	71
Lilliquist, D., Atl.*	8	10	3.97	32	165.2	202	34	79
Maddux, G., Chi. 19		12	2.95	35	238.1	222	82	135
Maddux, M., Phi.	1	3	5.15	16	43.2	52	14	26
Magrane, J., St.L.* 18		9	2.91	34	234.2	219	72	127
Mahler, R., Cin.	9	13	3.83	40	220.2	242	51	102
Martinez, De., Mon. 16		7	3.18	34	232.0	227	49	142
Martinez, R., L.A.	6	4	3.19	15	98.2	79	41	89
McCament, R., S.F.	1	1	3.93	25	36.2	32	23	12
McDowell, R., N.Y.-Phil.	4	8	1.96	69	92.0	79	38	47
McGaffigan, A., Mon.	3	5	4.68	57	75.0	85	30	40
McWilliams, L., Phi.*	2	11	4.10	40	120.2	123	49	54
Morgan, M., L.A.	8	11	2.53	40	152.2	130	33	72
Mulholland, T., S.F.-Phi.*	4	7	4.92	25	115.1	137	36	66
Myers, R., N.Y.*	7	4	2.35	65	84.1	62	40	88
O'Neal, R., Phi.	0	1	6.23	20	39.0	46	9	29
Ojeda, B., N.Y.* 13		11	3.47	31	192.0	179	78	95
Ontiveros, S., Phi.	2	1	3.82	6	30.2	34	15	12
Parrett, J., Phi. 12		6	2.98	72	105.2	90	44	98
Pena, A., L.A.	4	3	2.13	53	76.0	62	18	75
Perez, P., Mon.	9	13	3.31	33	198.1	178	45	152
Perry, P., Chi.*	0	1	1.77	19	35.2	23	16	20
Pico, J., Chi.	3	1	3.77	53	90.2	99	31	38
Portugal, M., Hou.	7	1	2.75	20	108.0	91	37	86
Power, T., St.L.	7	7	3.71	23	97.0	96	21	43
Quisenberry, D., St.L.	3	1	2.64	63	78.1	78	14	37
Rasmussen, D., S.D.* 10		10	4.26	33	183.2	190	72	87
Reed, R., Pit.	1	4	5.60	15	54.2	62	11	34
Reuschel, R., S.F. 17		8	2.94	32	208.1	195	54	111

Pitcher and Club	W	L	ERA	G	IP	H	BB	SO
Rhoden, R., Hou.	2	6	4.28	20	96.2	108	41	41
Rijo, J., Cin.	7	6	2.84	19	111.0	101	48	86
Robinson, D., S.F.	12	11	3.43	34	197.0	184	37	96
Robinson, J., Pit.	7	13	4.58	50	141.1	161	59	95
Robinson, R., Cin.	5	3	3.35	15	83.1	80	28	36
Ruffin, B., Phi.*	6	10	4.44	24	125.2	152	62	70
Sanderson, S., Chi.	11	9	3.94	37	146.1	155	31	86
Schatzeder, D., Hou.*	4	1	4.45	36	56.2	64	28	46
Schiraldi, C., Chi.-S.D. ...	6	7	3.51	59	100.0	72	63	71
Scott, M., Hou. 20		10	3.10	33	229.0	180	62	172
Scudder, S., Cin.	4	9	4.49	23	100.1	91	61	66
Searage, R., L.A.*	3	4	3.53	41	35.2	29	18	24
Sebra, B., Phi.-Cin.	2	3	5.20	21	55.1	65	28	35
Show, E., S.D.	8	6	4.23	16	106.1	113	39	66
Smiley, J., Pit.* 12		8	2.81	28	205.1	174	49	123
Smith, B., Mon. 10		11	2.84	33	215.2	177	54	129
Smith, D., Hou.	3	4	2.64	52	58.0	49	19	31
Smith, P., Atl.	5	14	4.75	28	142.0	144	57	115
Smith, Z., Atl.-Mon.*	1	13	3.49	48	147.0	141	52	93
Smoltz, J., Atl. 12		11	2.94	29	208.0	160	72	168
Sutcliffe, R., Chi. 16		11	3.66	35	229.0	202	69	153
Tekulve, K., Cin.	0	3	5.02	37	52.0	56	23	31
Terrell, W., S.D.	5	13	4.01	19	123.1	134	26	63
Terry, S., St.L.	8	10	3.57	31	148.2	142	43	69
Tewksbury, B., St.L.	1	0	3.30	7	30.0	25	10	17
Thompson, R., Mon.	0	2	2.18	19	33.0	27	11	15
Valdez, S., Atl.	1	2	6.06	19	32.2	31	17	26
Valenzuela, F., L.A.* 10		13	3.43	31	196.2	185	98	116
Viola, F., N.Y.*	5	5	3.38	12	85.1	75	27	73
Walk, B., Pit. 13		10	4.41	33	196.0	208	65	83
Wetteland, J., L.A.	5	8	3.77	31	102.2	81	34	96
Whitson, E., S.D. 16		11	2.66	33	227.0	198	48	117
Williams, M., Chi.*	4	4	2.76	76	81.2	71	52	67
Wilson, S., Chi.*	6	4	4.20	53	85.2	83	31	65
Wilson, T., S.F.*	2	3	4.35	14	39.1	28	24	22
Worrell, T., St.L.	3	5	2.96	47	51.2	42	26	41
Youmans, F., Phi.	1	5	5.70	10	42.2	50	25	20

BRUCE WEBER PICKS
HOW THEY'LL FINISH IN 1990

American League East

1. Boston
2. Milwaukee
3. Toronto
4. Cleveland
5. Baltimore
6. New York
7. Detroit

American League West

1. Kansas City
2. Oakland
3. California
4. Minnesota
5. Texas
6. Seattle
7. Chicago

National League East

1. New York
2. St. Louis
3. Chicago
4. Pittsburgh
5. Philadelphia
6. Montreal

National League West

1. San Diego
2. San Francisco
3. Cincinnati
4. Los Angeles
5. Houston
6. Atlanta

American League Champions: Kansas City
National League Champions: San Diego
World Champions: San Diego

YOU PICK
HOW THEY'LL FINISH IN 1990

**American League
East**

1.

2.

3.

4.

5.

6.

7.

**American League
West**

1.

2.

3.

4.

5.

6.

7.

**National League
East**

1.

2.

3.

4.

5.

6.

**National League
West**

1.

2.

3.

4.

5.

6.

American League Champions:

National League Champions:

World Champions: